The Temptation of Christ

The Temptation of Christ

Thomas Manton

Christian Focus Publications

Introduction © Maurice Roberts
Text © Christian Focus Publicatiuons

ISBN 1 85792 226 3

Published in 1996 by
Christian Focus Publications Ltd.
Geanies House, Fearn, Ross-shire,
IV20 1TW, Scotland, Great Britain.

Cover design by Donna Macleod

Printed and bound in Great Britain by
The Guernsey Press Co. Ltd., Vale, Guernsey, C.I.

CONTENTS

INTRODUCTION by Maurice Roberts 7

CHAPTER 1 21

CHAPTER 2 38

CHAPTER 3 57

CHAPTER 4 77

CHAPTER 5 106

CHAPTER 6 129

CHAPTER 7 149

INTRODUCTION

The book which the reader now has in his hands is an exposition of the Temptations of the Lord Jesus Christ as these are recorded for us in the Gospels of the New Testament scripture. These studies, or discourses, to use the word in vogue at the time when they were first written, were originally prepared by their distinguished author as outlines of sermons to be delivered in the pulpit. This fact will explain to the reader who is unfamiliar with the sermonic literature of the Puritan period why the writer of this book has set his material out in a rather unfamiliar way, with divisions and subdivisions.

Any such unfamiliarity of form and presentation, it needs to be said, is quickly forgotten once the reader begins to get into the book and its theme.

No subject is more relevant to our life in this world than how to cope with life's temptations and allurements. The world has always had these in plenty. But in this generation it may be truly stated that there are temptations innumerable which have to be faced and overcome. It is this practical reality which makes Thomas Manton's examination of the temptations of our Saviour immensely enlightening and helpful to the modern reader. Though some three centuries have elapsed since these sermons were first heard by their eager audiences, probably in London first, they are fresh and relevant in the highest degree. They throw valuable light on the nature and form of the Temptations of our Lord, on the subtlety of the devil and on the right way in which we are to resist the devil when he assails our faith as Christians today.

The Puritans of seventeenth-century Britain (and here the writer would include the Scottish as well as of the English divines of the period) were by common consent a most remarkable body of men. No less an authority on historical matters than Lord Macaulay could say of them that they were: 'Perhaps the most remarkable body of men which the world has ever produced.' The learned and celebrated Erasmus of Rotterdam, is said to have expressed his enthusiasm for the English Puritans in this way: 'O sit anima mea cum Puritanis Anglicanis!' (O let my soul be with the English Puritans!) The great J C Ryle, first Bishop of Liverpool, estimated their contribution in the following terms: 'The Puritans, as a body, have done more to elevate the national character than any class of Englishmen that ever lived.'

Such praise is high praise indeed. But it is no more than the sober truth. For the genius of Puritanism was just this: to live unto God and to instill into the hearts of men that God is to be set first in every aspect of man's life in this world: in the private life; and in the family, church and state. In Puritanism therefore we have a Christianity which aims to be thoroughly and consistently biblical in every aspect of man's life. And the engine which drove this concept of man's life on earth was the Puritan pulpit.

Among Puritan pulpit giants, none was more esteemed than Thomas Manton, the author of these sermons. If proof of this assertion were needed it could be given at length. Perhaps it will suffice in this context to say that the most formative and representative of all the documents produced in the Puritan age was published with a commendatory Epistle from Thomas Manton. We refer here to the Westminster Confession and the two accompanying Catechisms – documents which have gone through the earth and which have helped to shape the character of churches and nations. It is Dr Manton's name which appears at the end of the original Preface to these monumental theological writings. Clearly, Manton was deemed by his fellows in that theologically literate age to be the fittest person to recommend the Westminster standards to the Christian public at large. No single fact could more fully demonstrate the esteem in which he was then held. This should not surprise us, for it was said of Manton that he never preached a poor sermon!

Thomas Manton

Manton was born in Somersetshire, in the year 1620. Educated at Wadham College, Oxford, he was admitted to deacon's orders by Bishop Joseph Hall (later of Norwich), but he never took ordination as a 'priest' because he judged that he had been 'properly ordained' to the ministerial office. He commenced his ministry at Stoke Newington near London, and then took a charge in the city of London itself as successor to Obadiah Sedgewich, at Covent Garden.

During the Commonwealth period he was one of Cromwell's chaplains and offered the prayer at the latter's installation in 1657. At this period he preached frequently before Parliament.

At the Restoration he welcomed Charles II to the throne in 1660 and took part in the famous Savoy Conference. However in 1662 he was deprived of his living along with two thousand other ministers of Puritan conviction who, with Manton, were sufferers for conscience under the Act of Uniformity of that year.

When Manton then began to preach in his own rooms he

was arrested. The imprisonment which followed was not as severe as that suffered by many of the other Puritan preachers ejected from their pulpits by the 1662 Act. He was in fact permitted to preach to a small gathering of persons who came to his prison.

Thomas Manton passed to his eternal rest on October 18th 1677, at the age of fifty seven. He was buried at Stoke Newington and the funeral sermon was preached by a fellow Puritan minister of great fame, Dr William Bates.

Biographical details of Manton's life are few. Suffice to say that he was incessant in the ministerial labours which he loved and in which he excelled. His collected writings (including an index) comprise twenty two volumes of closely printed sermons. The seven sermons which make up this little volume are therefore but a small fragment of the total output of this learned and prolific preacher, of whom it could truly be said that from his own day until ours 'his praise is in all the churches'.

Manton must be called a 'preacher's preacher'. He has had a formative influence on those who have excelled since his day in the great work of the pulpit. George Whitefield, for instance, and C H Spurgeon had a high regard for Manton, as also did Dr D Martyn Lloyd-Jones. 'Manton's work is most commendable,' says Spurgeon, in reference to the volumes of sermons on Jude. The comment is typical.

It must be a significant tribute too to the honour and worth of Manton that he is currently in print in two editions, one American and the other British. All over the world he is being read today and is being increasingly appreciated as a 'master in Israel' in his ability to open out the riches of Holy Scripture.

To begin to read the great Puritan writers like Owen,

Sibbes, Flavel, Brooks and Manton is to enter into a world of thought and spirituality which it is almost impossible to find in other writers. This is not to overstate the case. Indeed, to 'discover' the Puritans can be almost to feel that they are, as a friend of the writer's once put it, 'more spiritual than the Bible itself'! This of course is an impossibility. But what is meant by those who have this experience is that they have come to discover that the Bible is a far more wonderful book than they had before realised.

To say what we have just said requires some explanation of how the standard Puritan writers, whose names we have given examples of above, came to be so eminent in their ability to open out the treasures of the Word of God.

For one thing, the Puritans (and here it is in place to state that Thomas Manton was in the ripe third generation) were brought up to love and to learn the Bible with 'their mother's milk'. Their writings abound with a profusion of biblical references from every part of the Word of God. For the Puritan mind a clear text from the Bible settled all controversy. Happily, they lived in that 'pre-critical age' when it had not yet become the habit of theologians and preachers to question the authority or the divine origin and sufficiency of scripture. The finality and inerrancy of the Bible were to them an unquestioned assumption, just as they ought to be ours. All that they believed therefore was tested by scripture and proved by scripture. What the Bible did not teach they did not include among articles of their faith. What scripture taught was to them binding, whether for faith or life, or both.

Then, we must appreciate that the mainline Puritans, of whom Manton was one *par excellence*, were committed to the Augustinian or Calvinistic system of theology. This underlying acceptance of the teachings of John Calvin as the true theology of the Bible was taken by them for granted. Of course they might differ on secondary matters. But they were of one mind in their commitment to what we now call 'Westminster' theology.

Thirdly, among reasons why they were so profound in their preaching, we must state that they excelled in practical and experimental religion. By this is meant that they made a close study of the human heart and its spiritual working as well as of the pastoral problems which they found among their hearers, both converted and otherwise; that they applied themselves to understand the wiles and methods of the devil; and that they viewed this life, as no Christians before or since have done better, as a time of probation and preparation for eternity.

To the above observations ought too to be added another: the Puritan way of looking at the Moral Law. As evangelicals, of course, they knew that salvation is by grace and through faith alone in Christ. But they were of the belief that the Ten Commandments have a place of great importance in the life of the believer since they are the rule for life in this world. We are not 'under the law' as a covenant of life, as they would put it. But we are as Christians under the Moral Law as a rule to show us how to glorify and enjoy God. No analysis of the religion of these men is adequate which does not take full account of this element in their thinking.

They would regard as Antinomian the forms of recent evangelicalism which fail to give a place to the Moral Law which we have described here. All thought that we are saved to enjoy an undefined 'freedom', as some modern writers have put it, would be anathema to them. Their love was to live 'by rule'. This did not mean that they taught salvation by the law, as we have said already. But it did mean that they insisted that the believer is to spend his energies in understanding how to please God in every way. In so doing he must work out the implication of the Decalogue. That this was their view is clear from the place they give to the Moral Law in their writings. They have been accused by some of being 'legalists'. But they were in fact no such thing. They were orthodox, evangelical believers, who lived to glorify and enjoy God.

The seven sermons which go to make up this book are, as we have seen, a short series of expositions on the Temptations of Christ. However, because the Puritan pulpit aimed above all else to speak to the heart and to arm the believer for the battle of faith, these sermons take on the character of a practical treatise showing us how we too are to resist the enemy of souls. That is not to say that these sermons spend little time on Christ's encounter with the tempter. That would be to do them an injustice, for they give most helpful insight into this subject.

The point we are now making is this rather. Manton, like Bunyan later and like his contemporary William Gurnall, is not attempting here just to elucidate the mysterious conflict between Satan and Christ, but to teach us along the way how our Lord's method is the only successful method in the fight against the devil. Our Saviour fights for himself. Yet he also fights for us, and to teach us how we also must fight in this same warfare.

Warning against the devil was a theme of the utmost importance to the seventeenth century preacher. On this subject they were masters. We today may well regard ourselves as but pygmies beside them when it comes to pastoral counselling.

There was in the genius of Puritanism an instinctive aptitude for pithy and memorable expressions. Perhaps this was the fruit of their mastery of the Latin writers, who formed a chief element in the educational system of their day. But, however it was, they were masters of the epigram and the memorable phrase. A few examples will help us to appreciate what is here meant.

Speaking of the wonderful doctrine that angels and men are taken into the family of God (Ephesians 1:10), Manton writes: 'Men by adoption, angels by transition, are taken into the family of Christ' (p. 173). Referring to the end of a period of temptation in a believer's life he writes: 'It will come in the best time when it cometh in God's time, neither too soon nor too late; it will come sooner than your enemies would have it, sooner than second causes would seem to promise; sooner than you deserve, soon enough to discover the glory of God to you ...'(p.160). 'Temptations of the right hand are more dangerous than those of the left' (p. 112). To work out that phrase the reader must go the place for himself! In giving us relief from our temptations God 'may love us, and yet delay our help'(p. 104). The Puritan abhorrence of human autonomy rings through in this passage surely: 'They that tempt God cast away God's rule (the Bible), and God's terms and obedience, and make others to themselves. The question is, whether God shall direct us, or we him?' (p. 96). In correcting those Christians who expect to feel rich emotions every time they come to the means of grace he wisely says: 'They suppose they must be fed with spiritual dainties, and overflow with sensible consolation in every holy duty, or else they are filled with disquieting thoughts about their acceptance with God' (pp. 89-90). Perhaps the following quotation, which must here be our last, is a summary of the whole book: 'Christians, you have not to do with a foolish devil, who will appear in his own colours and ugly shape, but with a devout devil, who, for his own turn, can pretend to be godly' (p. 61).

The question might occur to the mind of one not familiar with the Puritan writers: Why should a volume of sermons as old as this be republished today when there must surely be many books on this subject which are up-to-date and which deal with the same theme? The answer to this, in the opinion of the present writer, can be summed up in one word: profundity.

There is a depth of treatment here which will be very difficult indeed to match, whether in terms of biblical knowledge or of an understanding of the human heart with its proneness to fall into the snares of Satan. After all is said and done, there is no reason for us to imagine that the people of this modern world are any better at fighting the devil than our fathers were in the seventeenth century! Observation suggests indeed that we are a good deal less so. We are a technically expert age but we have not the remotest idea of how to go about the basic duties of life: marriage, social justice and the love of God. We live in a world which has been aptly called a 'Techtopia'. There is today everything to live with, but almost nothing to live for. It is there that the Puritans have so much to teach us. At the point at which we are so weak, they were strong. Our design in life, they would tell us, should be to live unto and upon God.

A few words must be said about the best way to read the Puritans. In this edition the reader will find that difficult words have been explained by the use of square brackets, in which the best modern equivalent word or term is given. The editor is solely responsible for these suggestions and he will have to bear the blame where it can be shown that he has missed the true meaning. However he believes that at least in most cases he has given the true sense of an obscure word. Here and there in the book Manton uses Greek, Latin and Hebrew words which in the original appear in their respective alphabets. Here it has been thought best to give these words in the approximate English transliteration and to place a translation after them. Obscure historical references too have been elucidated by a footnote.

How to read the Puritans

1. The reader must understand that this Puritan discourse was a series of sermons preached on a passage of scripture. The preacher's aim was to open up the meaning of the passage in its setting; and then to show his audience the principles which are of permanent validity; and finally to point to the practical lessons which the believer should attempt to apply in his own life.

2. The opening sentences are usually brief. They give the main headings of the passage and indicated originally to the hearers the form in which the preacher would divide up the text. This analysis is worth taking a little time over. Once its outline is grasped the reader can go ahead confident that he knows the general direction of the preacher's thoughts.

3. The early part of each sermon consists very much of an expression of the precise nature of the particular temptation under discussion. The opinions of other writers come in at this stage. Manton then sets out which of the proffered opinions he favours. This first part of each sermon is like a Bible study. Many modern preachers might be happy to go this far but might go no further.

4. However the meat of each sermon is to expound and to demonstrate the many ways in which Satan turns his subtlety and craft now this way and now that in an effort to deceive and to seduce the soul of man.

5. The points made at the end of each sermon under the heading of 'Uses' are the practical ways in which the author believes that the passage which he has expounded demands to be worked out by Christians in their everyday lives. Often such thoughts are put down in a seminal form. No doubt the preacher developed these points more fully in the course of his spontaneous remarks in the pulpit. A sermon after all is a thing of life and not a set piece to be read in the pulpit.

It is believed that the above guidelines will be of some assistance to the reader who may not have ventured before into our older spiritual literature. We wish him well as he now sets off. If there are initial difficulties arising from unfamiliarity of language or of style, let him remember that there are also treasure islands ahead for him and a vast store of spiritual gold to be carried off by the time the end is reached!

Maurice Roberts
Greyfriars Manse
Inverness
August 1995

The Temptation of Christ

TO THE READER[1]

The following discourse on this important subject of the temptation of our blessed Saviour, has been carefully perused, and transcribed from the reverend author's own manuscripts, are now, at the earnest request of divers [several] persons that were the happy auditors thereof [hearers of them], offered to public view. Had the author lived to publish these himself, they had come forth into the world more exact [polished]; but yet as they are now left, I doubt not but they will be very acceptable to all that have discerning minds, for the peculiar excellency contained in them.

Thus much was thought necessary to be said by way of preface, the work sufficiently commending itself, especially coming from such an author as Dr. Manton.

---

1. This treatise is found in Vol. I of the Collected Writings of Manton, beginning on p.257. The original wording has been slightly altered for this edition. Ed.

1

Then was Jesus led up of the Spirit into the wilderness, to be tempted of the devil
(Matthew 4:1).

This scripture giveth us the history of Christ's temptation, which I shall go over by degrees [gradually]. In the words observe: (1) The parties [persons] tempted and tempting. The person tempted was the *Lord Jesus Christ*. The person tempting was *the devil*. (2) The occasion inducing this combat, *Jesus was led up of the Spirit*. (3) The time, *then*. (4) The place, the *wilderness*.

From the whole observe: The Lord Jesus Christ was pleased to submit himself to an extraordinary combat with the tempter, for our good. (1) I shall explain the nature and circumstances of this extraordinary combat. (2) The reasons why Christ submitted to it. (3) The good of this to us.

1. The circumstances of this extraordinary combat. And here:

1. The persons combating.
Jesus and the devil, the seed of the woman and the seed of the serpent. It was designed long before: 'I will put enmity between thee and the woman, and between thy seed and her seed: it shall bruise thy head, and thou shalt bruise his heel' (Genesis 3:15); and now it is accomplished. Here is the Prince of Peace against the prince of darkness, Michael and the dragon, the Captain of our salvation and our grand enemy. The devil is the great architect of wickedness, as

Christ is the Prince of life and righteousness. These are the combatants: the one ruined the creation of God, and the other restored and repaired it.

2. *The manner of the combat.*
It is not merely a phantasm [unreal dream] that Christ was thus assaulted and used: no, he was tempted in reality, not in conceit and imagination only. It seemeth to be in the spirit, though it was real; as Paul was taken up into the third heaven, whether in the body or out of the body we cannot easily judge, but real it was. I shall more accurately discuss this question afterwards in its more proper place.

3. *What moved him; or How was he brought to enter into the lists with Satan?*
He was 'led by the Spirit', meaning thereby the impulsion [impulse] and excitation of the Holy Spirit, the Spirit of God. For it is said, 'Jesus, being full of the Holy Ghost, returned from Jordan, and was led by the Spirit into the wilderness' (Luke 4:1). He did not voluntarily put himself upon temptation but, by God's appointment, went up from Jordan farther into the desert.

We learn hence:
(1) That temptations come not by chance, not out of the earth, nor merely from the devil; but God ordereth them for his own glory and our good. Satan was fain to beg leave to tempt Job: 'And the LORD said unto Satan, Behold, all that he hath is in thy power, only upon himself put not forth thine hand' (Job 1:12); there is a concession with a limitation. Till God exposeth us to trials, the devil cannot trouble us, nor touch us. So Luke 22:31, 'Simon, Simon, Satan hath desired

to have you, that he may sift you as wheat.' Nay, he could not enter into the herd of swine without a patent [permit] and new pass [permission] from Christ: 'So the devils besought him, saying, If thou cast us out, suffer us to go away into the herd of swine' (Matthew 8:31).

This cruel spirit is held in the chains of an irresistible providence, that he cannot molest any creature of God without his permission; which is a great satisfaction to the faithful: all things which concern our trial are determined and ordered by God. If we be free, let us bless God for it, and pray that he would not 'lead us into temptation': if tempted, when we are in Satan's hands, remember Satan is in God's hand.

(2) Having given up ourselves to God, we are no longer to be at our own dispose and direction, but must submit ourselves to be led, guided, and ordered by God in all things. So it was with Christ, he was led by the Spirit continually: if he retire into the desert, he is 'led by the Spirit' (Luke 4:1); if he come back again into Galilee, 'Jesus returned in the power of the Spirit into Galilee' (Luke 4:4). The Holy Ghost leadeth him into the conflict, and when it was ended leadeth him back again. Now there is a perfect likeness [genuine similarity] between a Christian and Christ: he is led by the Spirit off and on, so we must be guided by the same Spirit in all our actions: 'For as many as are led by the Spirit of God, they are the sons of God' (Romans 8:14).

(3) That we must observe our warrant and calling in all we resolve upon. To put ourselves upon hazards [dangers] we are not called unto, is to go out of bounds to meet a temptation, or to ride into the devil's quarters [territory]. Christ did not go of his own accord into the desert, but by

divine impulsion [impulse], and so he came from thence. We may, in our place and calling, venture ourselves, on the protection of God's providence, upon obvious temptations; God will maintain and support us in them; that is to trust God; but to go out of our calling is to tempt God.

(4) Compare the words used in Matthew and Mark 1:12: 'And immediately the Spirit driveth him into the wilderness.' That shows that it was a forcible motion, or a strong impulse, such as he could not easily resist or refuse, so here is freedom – he was *led*; there is force and efficacious impression – he was *driven*, with a voluntary condescension thereunto. There may be liberty of man's will, yet the victorious efficacy of grace united together: a man may be taught and drawn, as Christ here was led, and driven by the Spirit into the wilderness.

2. The time
(1) *Presently after his baptism.*
Now the baptism of Christ agreeth with ours as to the general nature of it. Baptism is our initiation into the service of God, or our solemn consecration of ourselves to him; and it doth not only imply work, but fight: 'Neither yield ye your members as instruments [*hopla*, weapons] of unrighteousness unto sin; but yield yourselves unto God, as those that are alive from the dead, and your members as instruments of righteousness unto God' (Romans 6:13); and 'Let us cast off the works of darkness, and let us put on the armour of light' (Romans 13:12). Christ's baptism had the same general nature with ours, not the same special nature; the general nature is an engagement to God, the special use of baptism is to be a seal of the new covenant, or to be to us 'the baptism

of repentance for the remission of sins'. Now this Christ was not capable of, he had no sin to be repented of or remitted; but his baptism was an engagement to the same military work to which we are engaged. He came into the world for that end and purpose, to war against sin and Satan; he engageth as [takes on the task of being] the General, we as the common soldiers. He as the General: 'For this purpose the Son of God was manifested [*hina lusei*, to destroy], that he might destroy the works of the devil' (1 John 3:8). His baptism was the taking of the field as General; we undertake to fight under him in our rank and place.

(2) At this baptismal engagement *the Father had given him a testimony by a voice from heaven*: 'This is my beloved Son, in whom I am well pleased'; and the Holy Ghost had descended upon him in the form of a dove (Mark 3:16, 17). Now presently after this he is set upon by the tempter. Thus many times the children of God, after solemn assurances of his love, are exposed to great temptations. Of this you may see an instance in Abraham: 'And it came to pass after these things, that God did tempt Abraham' (Genesis 22:1); that is, after he had assured Abraham that he was 'his shield, and his exceeding great reward', and given him so many renewed testimonies of his favour. So Paul, after his rapture, 'lest he should be exalted above measure through the abundance of revelations, there was given to him a thorn in the flesh, the messenger of Satan to buffet him' (2 Corinthians 12:7). So Hebrews 10:32: 'But call to remembrance the former days, in which, after ye were illuminated, ye endured a great fight of afflictions'; i.e. after ye were fully convinced of the Christian faith, and furnished with those virtues and graces

that belong to it. God's conduct is gentle, and proportioned to our strength, as Jacob drove as the little ones were able to bear it. He never suffers his castle to be besieged till they are victualled [provided with food].

(3) *Immediately before he entered upon his prophetical office.*
Experience of temptations fits for the ministry, as Christ's temptations prepared him to set a-foot the kingdom of God, for the recovery of poor souls out of their bondage into the liberty of the children of God: verse 17, 'From that time Jesus began to preach, and to say, Repent, for the kingdom of heaven is at hand.' Our state of innocency was our health, the grace of the Redeemer our medicine, Christ our physician; for the devil had poisoned our human nature. Therefore, when he sets a-foot [starts off] his healing cure, it was fit and congruous [appropriate] that he should experimentally feel the power of the tempter, and in what manner he doth assault and endanger souls: Christ also would show us that ministers should not only be men of science [knowledge], but of experience.

(4) *The place or field where this combat was fought, the wilderness, where were none but wild beasts.*
'And he was there in the wilderness forty days tempted of Satan, and was with the wild beasts; and the angels ministered unto him' (Mark 1:13). Great question there is in what wilderness Christ was; their opinion is most probable who think it was the great wilderness, called the desert of Arabia, in which the Israelites wandered forty years, and in which Elijah fasted forty days and forty nights. In this solitary place Satan tried his utmost power against our Saviour.

This teacheth us:

(1) That Christ alone grappled with Satan, having no fellow-worker with him, that we may know the strength of our Redeemer, who is able himself to overcome the tempter without any assistance, and to 'save to the uttermost all that come unto God by him' (Hebrews 7:25).

(2) That the devil often abuseth [attacks] our solitude [when we are alone]. It is good sometimes to be alone; but then we need to be stocked with holy thoughts or employed in holy exercises, that we may be able to say, as Christ in John 16:32, 'I am not alone, because the Father is with me.' Howsoever [However,] a state of retirement from human converse [company], if it be not necessary, exposeth us to temptations; but if we are cast upon it, we must expect God's presence and help.

(3) That no place is privileged [exempt] from temptations, unless we leave our hearts behind us. David, walking on the terrace or house-top, was ensnared by Bathsheba's beauty (2 Samuel 11:2-4). Lot, that was chaste in Sodom, yet committed incest in the mountain, where there were none but his own family (Genesis 19:30, 31, etc). When we are locked in our closets, we cannot shut out Satan.

2. The reasons why Christ submitted to it.

(1) *With respect to Adam*, that the parallel between the first and second Adam might be more exact. They are often compared in scripture, as Romans 5, latter end [final verses], and 1 Corinthians 15; and we read in Romans 5:14 that the first Adam was *typos tou mellontos*, 'the figure of him that was to come'. And as in other respects, so in this; in the same way we were destroyed by the first Adam, in the same way we were restored by the second. Christ recovereth and winneth that which Adam lost. Our happiness was lost by

the first Adam being overcome by the tempter; so it must be recovered by the second Adam, the tempter being overcome by him. He that did conquer must first be conquered, that sinners might be rescued from the captivity wherein he held them captive. The first Adam, being assaulted quickly after his entrance into paradise, was overcome; and therefore must the second Adam overcome him as soon as he entered upon his office, and that in a conflict hand-to-hand, in that nature that was foiled [beaten]. The devil must lose his prisoners in the same way that he caught them. Christ must do what Adam could not do. The victory is gotten by the public person[2] in our nature [Christ], before it can be gotten by each individual in his own person, for so it was lost. Adam lost the day before he had any offspring, so Christ winneth it in his own person before he doth solemnly begin to preach the gospel and call disciples; and therefore here was the great overthrow of the adversary.

(2) *In regard of Satan*, who by his conquest got a twofold power over man by tempting, he got an interest in his heart to lead him 'captive at his will' and pleasure (2 Timothy 2:26); and he was made God's executioner, he got a power to punish him: 'That through death he might destroy him that had the power of death, that is, the devil' (Hebrews 2:14). Therefore, the Son of God, who interposed on our behalf, and undertook the rescue of sinners, did assume the nature of man, that he might conquer Satan in the nature that was conquered, and also offer himself as a sacrifice in the same nature for the demonstration of the justice of God.

---

2. In theology, Adam and Christ are called Public Persons because they were both Covenant-Heads, and so acted for others.

First, Christ must overcome by obedience, tried to the uttermost by temptations; and then he must also overcome by suffering. By overcoming temptations, he doth overcome Satan as a tempter; and by death he overcame him as a tormentor, or as the prince of death, who had the power of executing God's sentence. So that you see before he overcame him by merit, he overcame him by example, and was an instance of a tempted man before he was an instance of a persecuted man, or one that came to make satisfaction to God's justice.

(3) *With respect to the saints*, who are in their passage to heaven to be exposed to great difficulties and trials. Now that they might have comfort and hope in their Redeemer, and come to him boldly as one 'touched with a feeling of their infirmities', he himself submitted to be tempted.

This reason is recorded by the apostle in two places: 'For in that he himself hath suffered, being tempted, he is able to succour [help] them that are tempted' (Hebrews 2:18). Able to succour; that is, fit, powerful, inclined, effectually moved to succour them. None so merciful as those who have been once miserable; and they who have not only known misery, but felt it, do more readily relieve and succour others. God biddeth Israel to pity strangers:'Thou shalt neither vex a stranger, nor oppress him; for ye were strangers in the land of Egypt' (Exodus 22:21). They knew what it was to be exposed to the envy and hatred of the neighbours in the land where they sojourned: 'For ye know the heart of a stranger, seeing ye were strangers in the land of Egypt' (Exodus 23:9).

We read that when King Richard the First had been, on the sea near Sicily, like to be [in danger of being] drowned, he recalled that ancient and barbarous [pagan] custom, whereby the goods of shipwrecked men were escheated [sequestered] to the crown, making provision that those goods should be preserved for the right owners. Christ being tossed in the tempest of temptations, knows what belongs to the trouble thereof.

The other place is Hebrews 4:15: 'We have not an high priest which cannot be touched with the feeling of our infirmities, but was in all points tempted like as we are, yet without sin.' Christ hath experienced how strong the assailant [attacker] is, how feeble our nature is, how hard a matter it is to withstand when we are so sorely assaulted. His own experience of sufferings and temptations in himself doth entender his heart [make his heart tender], and make him fit for sympathy with us, and begets a tender compassion towards the miseries and frailties of his members.

(4) *With respect to Christ himself*, that he might be an exact pattern of obedience to God. The obedience is little worth, which is carried on in an even tenor [without trial], when we have no temptation to the contrary, but is cast off as soon as we are tempted to disobey: 'Blessed is the man that endureth temptation, for when he is tried, he shall receive the crown of life, which the Lord hath promised to them that love him' (James 1:12). And Hebrews 11:17: 'By faith Abraham, when he was tried, offered up Isaac: and he that had received the promises offered up his only-begotten son.' Now Christ was to be more eminent than all the holy ones of God, and therefore, that he might give an evidence of his piety, constancy, and trust in God, it was thought fit some trial should be made of him, that he might by example teach us what reason we have to hold to God against the strongest temptations.

3. The good of this to us. It teacheth us divers things, four I shall instance in.

(1) *To show us who is our grand enemy*, the devil, who sought the misery and destruction of mankind, as Christ did our salvation. And therefore he is called [ho echthros], *the enemy*; Matthew 13:39, 'The enemy that sowed them is the devil'. And he is called also [ho poneros], *the wicked one*, Matthew 13:19, as the first and deepest in evil. And because this malicious cruel spirit ruined mankind at first, he is called 'a liar and murderer from the beginning' (John 8:44). A liar, because of his deceit; a murderer, to show us what he hath done and would do. It was he that set upon Christ, and doth upon us, as at first to destroy our health, so still to keep us from our medicine and recovery out of the lapsed estate by the gospel of Christ.

(2) *That all men, none excepted, are subject to temptations.* If any might plead for exemption, our Lord Jesus, the eternal Son of God, might; but he was assaulted and tempted; and if the devil tempted our Saviour, he will be much more bold with us. The godly are yet in the way [journey], not at the end of the journey; in the field [of battle], not with the crown on their heads; and it is God's will that the enemy should have leave to assault them. None go to heaven without a trial: 'All these things are accomplished in your brethren that are in the flesh' (1 Peter 5:9). To look for an exempt privilege, or immunity from temptation, is to list ourselves as Christ's soldiers, and never expect battle or conflict.

(3) *It showeth us the manner of conflict, both of Satan's fight and our Saviour's defence.*
  (i) Of Satan's fight. It is some advantage not to be

ignorant of his enterprises: 'Lest Satan should get an advantage of us, for we are not ignorant of his devices' (2 Corinthians 2:11). Then we may the better stand upon our guard. He assaulted Christ by the same kind of temptations by which usually he assaults us. The kinds of temptations are reckoned up: 'The lusts of the flesh, the lusts of the eye, and the pride of life' (1 John 2:16). And James 3:15: 'This wisdom descendeth not from above, but is earthly, sensual, devilish.' With these temptations he assaulted our first parents: 'When the woman saw that the tree was good for fruit, and that it was pleasant to the eyes, and a tree to be desired to make one wise, she took of the fruit thereof, and did eat' (Genesis 3:8). And with the same temptations he assaulted Christ, tempting him to turn stones into bread, to satisfy the longings of the flesh; to fall down and worship him, as to the sight of a bewitching object to his eyes; to fly in the air in pride, and to get glory among men. Here are our snares, which we must carefully avoid.

(ii) The manner of Christ's defence, and so it instructeth us how to overcome and carry ourselves in temptations. And here are two things whereby we overcome:

By scripture. The word of God is 'the sword of the Spirit' (Ephesians 6:17), and 1 John 2:14: 'The word of God abideth in you, and ye have overcome the wicked one.' It is good to have the word of God abide in our memories, but chiefly in our hearts, by a sound belief and fervent love to the truth.

Partly by resolution: 'Arm yourselves with the same mind' (1 Peter 4:1), that is, that was in Christ. When Satan grew bold and troublesome, Christ rejects him with indignation. Now the conscience of our duty should thus prevail with us to be resolute therein; the double-minded are as it were torn in pieces between God and the devil: 'A double-minded man is unstable in all his ways'(James 1:8). Therefore, being in God's way, we should resolve to be deaf to all temptations.

(4) *The hopes of success.* God would set Christ before us as a pattern of trust and confidence, that when we address ourselves to serve God, we might not fear the temptations of Satan. We have an example of overcoming the devil in our glorious head and chief. If he pleaded: 'In the world ye shall have tribulation, but be of good cheer, I have overcome the world' (John 16:33); the same holdeth good here, for the enemies of our salvation are combined. He overcame the devil in our natures, that we might not be discouraged: we fight against the same adversaries in the same cause, and he will give power to us, his weak members, being full of compassion, which certainly is a great comfort to us.

Use.[3] Of instruction to us:
Use 1: *To reckon upon temptations.* As soon as we mind our baptismal covenant, we must expect that Satan will be our professed foe, seeking to terrify or allure us from the banner of our captain, Jesus Christ. Many, after baptism, fly to Satan's camp.

There are a sort of men in the visible church, who, though they do not deny their baptism, as those did: 'Who have forgotten that they were purged from their old sins' (2 Peter 2:9), yet they carry themselves as if they were in league with the devil, the world, and the flesh, rather than with the Father, Son, and Holy Ghost; with might and main they

---

3. 'Use' is the Puritan preacher's term for 'Application'. Ed.

oppose Christ's kingdom, both abroad and at home, in their own hearts, and are wholly governed by worldly things, the lusts of the flesh, and the lusts of the eye, and the pride of life. Now these are the devil's agents, and the more dangerous, because they use Christ's name against his offices, and the form of his religion to destroy the power thereof; as the dragon in the Revelation, pushed with the horns of the Lamb.

Others are not venomously and malignantly set against Christ, and his interest in the world, or in their own hearts, but tamely yield to the lusts of the flesh, and go 'like an ox to the slaughter, and a fool to the correction of the stocks' (Proverbs 7:22). We cannot say that Satan's work lieth about these. Satan needeth not besiege the soul by temptations; that is his already by peaceable possession; 'when a strong man armed keepeth his palace, his goods are in peace' (Luke 11:21). There is no storm when wind and tide goeth together.

But then there is a third sort of men, that begin to be serious, and to mind [be concerned about] their recovery by Christ; they have many good motions [feeling] and convictions of the danger of sin, excellency of Christ, necessity of holiness; they have many purposes to leave sin and enter upon a holy course of life, but 'the wicked one cometh, and catcheth away that which was sown in his heart' (Matthew 13:19). He beginneth betimes [at an early stage] to oppose the work, before we are confirmed and settled in a course of godliness, as he did set upon Christ presently upon his baptism. Baptism in us implieth avowed dying unto sin and living unto God; now God permitteth temptation to try our resolution. There is a fourth sort, of such as have made some progress in religion, even to a degree of eminency; these are not altogether free; for if the devil had confidence to assault the declared Son of God, will he be afraid of a mere mortal man? No; these he assaulteth many times very sorely: pirates venture on the greatest booty. These he seeketh to draw off from Christ, as Pharaoh sought to bring back the Israelites after their escape; or to foil them by some scandalous fall, to do religion a mischief: 'By this deed thou hast given great occasion to the enemies of the LORD to blaspheme' (2 Samuel 12:14); or at least to vex them and torment them, to make the service of God tedious and uncomfortable to them: Luke 22:31, 'Simon, Simon, behold, Satan hath desired to have you, that he might sift you as wheat' – to toss and vex you, as wheat in a sieve. So that no sort of Christians can promise themselves exemption; and God permitteth it, because to whom much is given, of them the more is required.

Use 2: The manner and way of his fight is by the world, *per blanda et aspera* [by easy and hard things], *by the good or evil things of the world*. There is 'armour of righteousness on the right hand and on the left' (2 Corinthians 6:7), as there are right-hand and left-hand temptations. Both ways he lieth in ambush in the creature. Sometimes he tempts us by the good things of the world: 'And Satan stood up against Israel, and provoked David to number Israel' (1 Chronicles 21:1), so glorying in his might, and puissance [power], and victory over neighbour kings. So meaner [lesser] people he tempteth to abuse their wealth to pride and luxury; therefore we are pressed to be sober: 'Be sober, be vigilant; because your adversary the devil, as a roaring lion, walketh about, seeking whom he may devour' (1 Peter 5:8). The devil maketh an advantage of our prosperity, to divert us from

God and heaven, and to render us unapt [unfit] for the strictness of our holy calling.

Sometimes he tempts us by the evil things of this world: 'Put forth thine hand now and touch all that he hath, and he will curse thee to thy face' (Job 1:11). Satan's aim in bringing the saints into trouble is to draw them to fretting, murmuring, despondency, and distrust of providence, yea, to open defection [departure] from God, or blasphemy against him; and therefore it is said in 1 Peter 5:9, 'Knowing that the same afflictions', etc., because temptations are conveyed to us by our afflictions or troubles in the flesh.

Use 3: *His end is to dissuade us from good, and persuade us to evil.* To dissuade us from good by representing the impossibility, trouble and small necessity of it.

If men begin to apply themselves to a strict course, such as they have sworn to in baptism, either it is so hard as not to be borne, as John 6:60: 'This is a hard saying, who can bear it?' Whereas, Matthew 19:29: 'Every one that hath forsaken houses, or brethren, etc, for my name's sake, shall receive an hundredfold, and shall inherit everlasting life.' Or the troubles which accompany a strict profession are many. The world will note us: 'Nevertheless, among the chief rulers also many believed on him; but because of the Pharisees, they did not confess him, lest they should be put out of the synagogue' (John 12:42). Whereas we must not be ashamed of Christ: 'If we suffer, we shall also reign with him; if we deny him, he also will deny us' (2 Timothy 2:12,). Or that we need not be so strict and nice [precise], whereas all we can do is little enough: 'Not so, lest there be not enough for us and you' (Matthew 25:9). In general, the greatest mischiefs done [to] us by sin are not regarded [noticed], but the least inconvenience that attendeth our duty is urged and aggravated. He persuadeth us to evil by profit, pleasure, necessity; we cannot live without it in the world. He hideth the hook, and showeth the bait only; he concealeth the hell, the horror, the eternal pains that follow sin, and only telleth you how beneficial, profitable, and delightful the sin will be to you: Proverbs 9:17, 18, 'Stolen waters are sweet, and bread eaten in secret is pleasant. But he knoweth not that the dead are there, and that her guests are in the depths of hell'.

Use 4: While we are striving against temptations, let us remember our General [Christ]. We do but follow the Captain of our salvation, who hath vanquished the enemy, and will give us the victory if we keep striving: 'The God of peace shall bruise Satan under your feet shortly' (Romans 16:2). Not *his* feet, but *ours*: we shall be conquerors. Our enemy is vigilant and strong. It is enough for us that our Redeemer is merciful and faithful in succouring the tempted, and able to master the tempter, and defeat all his methods. Christ hath conquered him, both as a lamb and as a lion (Revelation 5:5, 8). The notion of a lamb intimateth his sacrifice, the notion of a lion his victory: in the lamb is merit, in the lion strength; by the one he maketh satisfaction to God, by the other he rescueth sinners out of the paw of the roaring lion, and maintaineth his interest in their hearts. Therefore let us not be discouraged, but closely adhere to him.

2

And when he had fasted forty days and forty nights, he was afterwards an hungered. And when the tempter came to him, he said, If thou be the Son of God, command that these stones be made bread. And he answered and said, It is written, Man liveth not by bread alone, but by every word that proceedeth out of the mouth of God (Matthew 4:2-4).

In these words there are three branches: (1) The occasion; (2) The temptation itself; (3) Christ's answer.

1. The occasion of the first temptation, in the second verse, 'When he had fasted forty days and forty nights, he was afterwards an hungered'. Where take notice: (1) Of his fasting; (2) Of his hunger.

And something I shall speak of them conjunctly [both together], something distinctly and apart.

1. *Conjunctly*

In every part of our Lord's humiliation, there is an emission of some beams of his Godhead, that whenever he is seen to be true man, he might be known to be true God also. Is Christ hungry? There was a fast of forty days' continuance preceding, to show how, as God, he could sustain his human nature. The verity [reality] of his human nature is seen, because he submitted to all our sinless infirmities. The power of his divine nature was manifested, because it enabled him to continue forty days and nights without eating or drinking anything, the utmost that an ordinary man can fast being but nine days usually. Thus his divinity and humanity are expressed in most or all of his actions: 'The Word was made flesh, and dwelt among us, and we beheld his glory, the glory as of the only-begotten Son of God' (John 1:14).

There was a veil of flesh, yet the glory of his divine nature was seen, and might be seen, by all that had an eye and heart to see it. He lay in the manger at Bethlehem, but a star appeared to conduct the wise men to him; and angels proclaimed his birth to the shepherds (Luke 2:13, 14). He grew up from a child, at the ordinary rate of other children; but when he was but twelve years old, he disputed with the doctors (Luke 2:42). He submitted to baptism, but then owned by a voice from heaven to be God's beloved Son. He was deceived [disappointed of fruit] in the fig-tree when an hungered, which shows the infirmity of human ignorance; but, suddenly blasted [cursed], this [tree] manifested the glory of a divine power (Matthew 21:19). Here tempted by Satan, but ministered unto and attended upon by a multitude of glorious angels (Matthew 4:11); finally crucified through weakness, but living by the power of God (2 Corinthians 13:4). He hung dying on the cross; but then the rocks were rent, the graves opened, and the sun darkened.

All along you may have these intermixtures. He needed to humble himself to purchase our mercies; but withal [also] to give a discovery [revelation] of a divine glory to assure our faith. Therefore, when there were any evidences of human frailty, lest the world should be offended, and stumble thereat [at it], he was pleased at the same time to give some notable demonstration of the divine power; as, on the other side, when holy men are honoured by God, something falleth out to humble them (2 Corinthians 12:7).

2. *Distinctly and apart.* Where observe:

(1) That he fasted forty days and forty nights; so did Moses when he received the law (Exodus 34:28); and, at the restoring of the law, Elias did the like [likewise] (1 Kings 19:8). Now what these two great prophets had done, Christ, the great prophet and doctor of the Christian church, did also. For the number of forty days, curiosity may make itself work enough; but it is dangerous to make conclusions where no certainty appeareth. However this is not amiss, that forty days were the usual time allotted for repentance: as to the Ninevites (Jonah 3:4); so the prophet Ezekiel was to bear the sins of the people for forty days; and the flood was forty days in coming on the old world (Genesis 7:17). This was the time given for their repentance, and therefore for their humiliation; yet the forty days' fast in Lent is ill-grounded on this example, for this fast of Christ cannot be imitated by us, [any] more than [any] other [of] his miracles.

(2) At the end of the forty days he was an hungered, sorely assaulted with faintness and hunger, as any other man at any time is for want of meat [food]. God's providence permitted it, that he might be more capable of Satan's temptations; for Satan fits his temptations to men's present case and condition. When Christ was hungry, he tempteth him to provide bread, in such a way as the tempter doth prescribe. He worketh upon what he findeth: when men are full, he tempteth them to be proud and forget God; when they are destitute, to distrust God: if he sees men covetous, he fits [supplies] them with a wedge of gold, as he did Achan; if discontented and plotting the destruction of another, he findeth out occasions [for their discontent to be felt]. When Judas had a mind to sell his Master, he presently sendeth him a chapman [opportunity to do so]. Thus he doth

work upon our dispositions, or our condition; most upon our dispositions, but here only upon Christ's condition. He observeth which way the tree leaneth, and then thrusteth it forward.

2. The temptation itself (verse 3). Where two things are observable: (1) the intimation of his address, 'And when the tempter came to him'; (2) the proposal of the temptation, 'If thou be the Son of God', etc.

1. *For the address to the temptation*, 'And when the tempter came to him', there two things must be explained: (a) In what manner the tempter came to Christ; (b) How he is said to come then to him.

(1) *How he came to him*
Whether [are] the temptations of Christ to be understood by way of vision, or historically, as things visibly acted and done? This latter I incline unto; and I handle here, because it is said, 'The tempter came to him'. This importeth [implies] some local motion and accession [movement and approach] of the tempter to Christ, under a visible and external form and shape. As afterwards, when the Lord biddeth him be gone, 'then the devil leaveth him' (verse 11); a retiring of Satan out of his presence, not the ceasing of a vision only. Yea, all along, he 'taketh him', and 'sets him on a pinnacle of the temple', and 'taketh him to an high mountain'. All which show some external appearance of Satan, and not a word that intimateth a vision. Neither can it be conceived how any act of adoration could be demanded by Satan of Christ – 'fall down and worship me' – unless the object to be worshipped were set before him in some visible shape.

The coming of the angels to Christ when the devil left him (verse 11), all understand historically, and of some external coming. Why is not the coming and going of the devil thus to be understood also? And if all had been done in vision, and not by converse, how could Christ be an hungered, or the devil take that occasion to tempt him? How could answers and replies be tossed to and fro, and scriptures alleged [affirmed]? So that from the whole view of the frame of the text [taking all the evidence], here was some external congress [conversation] between Christ and the devil.

If you think it below Christ, you forget the wonderful condescension of the Son of God; it is no more unworthy of him than crucifixion, passion and burial was. It is true, in the writing of the prophets, many things historically related were only done in vision; but not in the Gospels, which are an history of the life and death of Christ; where things are plainly set down as they were done. To men the grievousness of Christ's temptations would be much lessened if we should think it only a piece of fantasy, and imaginary rather than real. And if his temptations be lessened, so will his victory, so will our comfort. In short, such as was Christ's journey into the wilderness, such was his fast, such his temptation; all were real. For all are delivered to us in the same style and thread of discourse.

Yea, further, if these things had been only in vision and ecstasy, there would have been no danger to Christ in the second temptation, when he was tempted to throw himself down from the pinnacle of the temple. Surely then he was *truly* tempted, and not in vision only; yea, it seemeth not so credible and agreeable to the dignity and holiness of Christ, that Satan should tempt by internal false suggestions, and the immission of species [visionary ideas] into his fancy or understanding; that Christ should seem to be here and there, when all the while he was in the desert. For either Christ took notice of these false images in his fancy, or not. If not, there is no temptation; if so, there will be an error in the mind of Christ, that he should think himself to be on the pinnacle of the temple, or top of an high mountain, when he was in the desert. It is hard to think these suggestions could be made without some error or sin; but an external suggestion maketh the sin to be in the tempter only, not in the person tempted. Our first parents lost not their innocency by the external suggestion, but internal admission of it, dwelling upon it in their minds. To a man void of sin, the tempter hath no way of tempting but externally.

(2) *How is this access to Christ said to be after his fasting*, when, in Luke 4:2, it is said, 'Being forty days tempted of the devil, and in those days he did eat nothing; and when they were ended, he afterward hungered'?

I answer: (i) Some conceive that the devil tempted Christ all the forty days, but then he tempted him invisibly, as he doth other men, striving to inject sinful suggestions; but he could find nothing in him to work upon (John 14:30). But at forty days' end he taketh another course, and appeareth visibly in the shape of an angel of light. He saith he came to him, most solemnly and industriously to tempt him. This opinion is probable.

(ii) It may be answered, Luke's speech must be understood: 'Being forty days in the wilderness, and in those days he did eat nothing, and was tempted'; that is, those days being ended. There is, by a prolepsis [looking ahead], some little inversion of the order. But because of Mark 1:13, where it is said, 'He was in the wilderness forty days, tempted of Satan, and was with the wild beasts', take the former answer.

2. *The proposal of the temptation*, 'If thou be the Son of God, command that these stones be made bread'.

Certainly every temptation of the devil tendeth to sin. Now where is the sin of this? If Christ had turned stones into bread, and declared himself by this miracle to be the Son of God, there seemeth to be no such evil in this. Like miracles he did upon other occasions; as turning water into wine at the marriage feast, multiplying the loaves in the distribution for feeding the multitude. Here was no curiosity; the fact seemed to be necessary to supply his hunger. Here is no superfluity [extravagance] urged – into 'bread', not dainties or occasions of wantonness, but 'bread' for his necessary sustenance. I answer, Notwithstanding all this fair appearance, yet this first assault which is propounded by Satan was very sore and grievous.

(1) *Because manifold [all sorts of] sins are implied in it, and there are many temptations combined in this one assault.*
(i) In that Christ, who was led by the Spirit into the wilderness to fast, and so to be tempted, must now break his fast and work a miracle at Satan's direction. The contest between God and the devil is, who shall be sovereign? therefore it was not meet [fitting] that Christ should follow the devil's advice, and do anything at his command and suggestion.

(ii) That Christ should doubt of that voice that he heard from heaven at his baptism, 'Thou art my beloved Son'; and the devil cometh, 'If thou be the Son of God'. That it should anew be put to trial by some extraordinary work, whether it were true of no, or he should believe it, yea or no [not]. No temptation so sore, no dart so poisonable [poisonous], as that which tendeth to [leads people to] the questioning of the grounds of faith; as this did the love of God, so lately spoken of him. Therefore this is one of the sharpest arrows that could come out of Satan's bow.

(iii) It tendeth to weaken his confidence in the care and love of God's fatherly providence; being now afflicted with hunger in the desert place, where no supply of food could be had, Satan would draw him to suspect and doubt of his Father's providence, as if it were incompatible to be the Son of God and to be left destitute of means to supply his hunger, and therefore must take some extraordinary course of his own to furnish himself.

(iv) It tended to put him upon an action of vainglory, by working a miracle before the devil, to show his power; as all needless actions are but a vain ostentation.

(2) *Because it was in itself a puzzling and perplexing proposal, not without inconveniences on both sides, whichsoever of the extremes our Lord should choose; whether he did, or did not, what the tempter suggested.*

If he did, he might seem to doubt of the truth of the oracle, by which he was declared to be the Son of God, or to distrust God's providence, or to give way to a vain ostentation of his own power. If he did not, he seemed to be wanting [to come short], in not providing necessary food for his sustentation when it was in his power to do so; and it seemed to be unreasonable to hide that which it concerned all to know, to wit, that he was the Son of God. And it seemeth grievous to hear others suspicious concerning ourselves, when it is in our power easily to refute them; such provocations can hardly be borne by the most modest spirits. This temptation was again put upon Christ on the cross: 'If thou be the Son of God, come down from the cross' (Matthew 27:40). But all is to be done at God's direction, and as it becometh our obedience to him, and respect to his glory. Satan and his instruments will be satisfied with no proofs of principles of faith, but such as he and they will prescribe, and which cannot be given without entrenching upon [weakening] our obedience to God, and those counsels which he hath wisely laid for his own glory.

And if God's children be surprised with such a disposition, it argueth so far the influence of Satan upon them, namely, when they will not believe but upon their own terms: as Thomas, 'Except I see in his hands the print of the nails, and put my finger into the print of the nails, and thrust my hand into his side, I will not believe' (John 20:25). If we will not accept of the graces of faith as offered by God, but will interpose conditions of our own prescribing, we make a snare to ourselves. God may in condescension to a weak believer grant what was his fault to seek, as he doth afterwards to Thomas (verse 27); but there is no reason he should grant it to the devil, he being a malicious and incorrigible [beyond hope of correction] spirit coming temptingly to ask it.

(3) *This temptation was cunning and plausible*; it seemed only to tend to Christ's good, his refection [refreshment] when hungry, and his honour and glory, that this might be a full demonstration of his being the Son of God.

There is an open solicitation to evil, and a covert; explicit and implicit; direct and indirect. This last here. It was not an open, direct, explicit solicitation to sin, but covert, implicit, and indirect, which sort of temptations are more dangerous. There was no need of declaring Christ's power by turning stones into bread before the devil, and at his instance and suit [request]. It was neither necessary nor profitable. Not necessary for Christ's honour and glory, it being sufficiently evidenced before by that voice from heaven, or might be evident to him without new proof. Nor was it necessary for Christ's refection [refreshment], because he might be sustained by the same divine power by which hitherto he had been supported for forty days. Nor was it profitable, none being present but the devil, who asked not this proof for satisfaction, but cavil [to be argumentative]; and that he might boast and gain advantage, if Christ had done anything at his instance and direction. And in this peculiar dispensation all was to be done by the direction of the Holy Spirit, and not the impure spirit. I come now to the third branch [division].

3. Christ's answer

'And he answered and said, It is written, Man liveth not by bread alone, but by every word that proceedeth out of the mouth of God' (verse 4).

Christ's answer is not made to that part of the proposal, 'If thou be the Son of God', but to the urgent necessity of his refection [refreshment]. The former was clear and evident, the force of the temptation lay not there; but the latter, which Satan sought to make most advantage of, is clearly refuted. Christ's answer is taken out of Deuteronomy 8:3; and this answer is not given for the tempter's sake, but ours, that we may know how to answer in like cases, and repel such kind of temptations. In the place quoted, Moses speaketh of manna, and showeth how God gave his people manna from heaven, to teach them that though bread be the ordinary means of sustaining man, yet God can feed him by other means, which he is pleased to make use of for that purpose. His bare word, or nothing; all cometh from his divine power and virtue, whatever he is pleased to give for the sustentation [support] of man, ordinary or extraordinary. The tempter had said that either he must die for hunger, or turn stones into bread. Christ showeth that there is a middle [golden mean] between both these extremes. There are other ways which the wisdom of God hath found out, or hath appointed by his word, or decreed to such an end, and maketh use of in the course of his providence. And the instance is fitly chosen; for he that provided forty years for a huge multitude in the desert, he will not be wanting to his own Son, who had now fasted but forty days. In the words there is:

(1) A concession or grant, that ordinarily man liveth by bread; and therefore must labour for it, and use it when it may be had.

(2) There is a restriction of the grant, that it is not by bread only: 'But by every word that proceedeth out of the mouth of God'. The business is to explain how a man can live by the word of God, or what is meant by it.

(i) Some take *word* for the word of precept, and expound it thus: if you be faithful to your duty, God will provide for you. For in every command of God, general or particular, there is a promise expressed or implied of all things necessary: 'Blessed shall be thy basket and thy store' (Deuteronomy 28:5); and 'Seek ye first the kingdom of God, and his righteousness, and all these things shall be added unto you' (Matthew 6:33). Now we may lean upon this word of God, keep ourselves from indirect means, and in a fair way of providence [by looking to God's providence] refer the issue to God.

(ii) Some take the *word* for the word of promise, which indeed is the livelihood of the saints: 'Thy testimonies have I taken as an heritage for ever; they are the rejoicing of my heart' (Psalm 119:111). God's people in a time of want can make a feast to themselves out of the promises; and when seemingly starved in the creature [food, etc.], fetch [obtain] not only peace and grace and righteousness, but food and raiment [clothing] out of the covenant.[4]

(iii) Rather, I think, it is taken for his providential word or commanded blessing; for as God made all things by his word, so 'he upholdeth all things by the word of his power' (Hebrews 1:3). His powerful word doth [accomplishes] all in the world: 'He sendeth forth his commandment on the earth; his word runneth very swiftly; he giveth snow like wool' (Psalm 147:15). And then, in the 18th verse, 'He sendeth out his word, and melteth them.' As the word of creation made all things, so the word of providence sustaineth all things. This word is spoken of in Psalm 107:20: 'He sent his word, and his word healed them; and delivered them from all their destructions.' It is *dictum factum* [a word done] with God; if he speak but the word, it is all done: 'Speak but the word, and thy servant shall be whole' (Matthew 8:8). So Luke 4:36: 'What a word is this! for with authority and power he commandeth the unclean spirits, and they come out'. So of Joseph it is said: 'Until the time that his word came; the word of the Lord tried him' (Psalm 105:19); that is, his power and influence on the hearts of the parties concerned for his deliverance. Well, then, the power of sustaining life is not in bread, but in the word of God; not

---

4. 'Covenant' is a term used in the older writers to refer to the gospel and all its promises, by which God guarantees to provide all that believers need.

in the means, but in God's commanded blessing, which may be conveyed to us by means, or without means, as God pleaseth. There is a powerful commanding word which God useth for health, strength, sustentation, or any effect wherein the good of his people is concerned. He is the great commander of the world. If he say to anything 'Go', it goeth; 'Come', and it cometh.

Thus you have the history of the first temptation.

Observations

Observe, first, *that God may leave his children and servants to great straits [difficulties]*; for Christ himself was sorely an hungered [very hungry]: so God suffereth [permits] his people to hunger in the wilderness before he gave them manna. Therefore it is said, 'He weakeneth the strength of the people in the way' (Psalm 102:23). He hath sundry trials [various tests] wherewith [by which] to exercise our faith, and sometimes by sharp necessities [acute shortage]. Paul and his companions had continued fourteen days, and had taken nothing (Acts 27:33). Many times God's children are thus tried: trading is dead [our income falls short], and there are many mouths to be fed, and little supply cometh in; yet this is to be borne [put up with]: none of us [will ever be] more poor than Christ, or more destitute than was Christ.

Secondly, *that the devil maketh [takes] an advantage of our necessities [needs]*. When Christ was an hungered, then the tempter came to him; so unto us. Three sorts of temptations he then useth to [to try] us, the same he did to Christ:

(1) Either he tempteth us to unlawful means to satisfy our hunger; so he did to Christ, who was to be governed by the Spirit, to work a miracle to provide for his bodily wants at

Satan's direction; so us. Poverty hath a train [string] of sinful temptations: 'Lest I be poor, and steal, and take the name of my God in vain' (Proverbs 30:9). Necessities are urging [when we are in need, we are under pressure], but we must not go to the devil for a direction how to supply ourselves, lest he draw us to put our hand to our neighbour's goods or to defraud our brother, or betray the peace of our conscience, or to do some unworthy thing, that we may live the more comfortably. You cannot plead necessity; it is to relieve your charge, to maintain life; God is able to maintain it in his own way. No necessity can make any sin warrantable. It is necessary thou shouldst not sin; it is not necessary thou shouldst borrow more than thou canst pay, or use any fraudulent means to get thy sustenance. If others be merciful, thou must not be unrighteous.

(2) To question our adoption, as he did the filiation of Christ[5]: 'If thou be the Son of God'. It is no wonder to find Satan calling in question the adoption and regeneration of God's children, for he calleth in question the filiation and sonship of the Son of God, though so plainly attested but a little before. 'Ye have forgotten the exhortation which speaketh unto you as children, My Son ...' (Hebrews 12:5). Certainly whatever moveth us to question our interest in God's fatherly love, bare afflictions should not; for to be without afflictions is a sign of bastards. God hath no illegitimate children, but God hath degenerate children, who are left to a larger discipline.

(3) To draw us to a diffidence [doubt] and distrust of God's providence: this he sought to breed in Christ, or at

---

5. A theological term: by 'filiation' is meant that eternal act of Christ within the Trinity by which He is the Son of God.

least to do something that might seem to countenance it, if he should upon his motion [i.e., Satan's suggestion] work a miracle. Certainly it is Satan's usual temptation to work in us a disesteem [distrust] of God's goodness and care, and to make us pore altogether upon [entirely taken up with] our wants. A sense of our wants may be a means to humble us, to quicken us to prayer; but it should not be a temptation to beget [create] in us unthankfulness, or murmuring against God's providence, or any disquietness or unsettledness in our minds. And though they may be very pinching [acute, severe], yet we should still remember that God is good to them that are of a clean heart (Psalm 73:1).

God hath in himself all-sufficiency, who knoweth both what we want, and what is fittest for us, and is engaged by his general providences as a faithful Creator: 'Let them that suffer according to the will of God, commit the keeping of their souls to him in well-doing, as unto a faithful Creator' (1 Peter 4:19); but more especially as related to us as a Father: 'Your heavenly Father knoweth that you have need of all these things' (Matthew 6:32). And by his faithful promise: 'He hath said, I will never leave thee, nor forsake thee' (Hebrews 13:5). And he will give us every good thing while we fear him: 'O fear the LORD, ye his saints: for there is no want to them that fear him. The young lions do lack and suffer hunger: but they that seek the Lord shall not want any good thing' (Psalm 34:9, 10). And walk uprightly: 'For the LORD God is a sun and a shield: the LORD will give grace and glory: no good thing will he withhold from them that walk uprightly' (Psalm 84:11). And seek it of him by prayer: 'Ask, and it shall be given you; seek, and ye shall find; knock, and it shall be opened unto you' (Matthew 7:11).

But you will say, You preach only to the poor and

destitute. I answer, I speak as my subject leadeth me: it will put the point generally; Satan maketh [takes] an advantage of our condition. Christ had power to do what was suggested; every condition hath its snares, a full condition most of all: 'Let their table be a snare, their welfare for a trap' (Psalm 69:22). He hideth his snares and gins [traps] to catch our souls. In all the comforts men enjoy that are apt to grow proud, to forget God, to become merciless to others who want what they enjoy; to live in vain pleasures, and to forget eternity; to live in sinful security, in the neglect of Christian duties; to be enslaved to sensual satisfactions, to be flat [unfeeling] and cold in prayer. This glut [excess] and fulness of worldly comforts is much more dangerous than our hunger.

Thirdly, observe, *in tempting, Satan pretendeth to help the tempted party [person] to a better condition*; as here he seemeth careful to have bread provided for Christ at his need, yea, pretendeth respect to his glory, and to have him manifest himself to be the Son of God, by such a miracle as he prescribeth. This seeming tenderness, counselling Christ to support his life and health, was the snare laid for him. Thus he dealt with our first parents: he seeketh to weaken the reputation of God's love and kindness to man, and to breed in the woman's mind a good opinion of himself. That his suggestions might make the greater impression upon her, he manageth all his discourse with her, that all the advice which he seemeth to give her proceeded of his love and good affection towards her and her husband, pretending a more than ordinary desire and care of man's good (Genesis 3:5), as if he could direct him how to become a match for God himself.

So still he dealeth with us; for alas! otherwise 'in vain is the snare laid in the sight of any bird' (Proverbs 1:17). He covereth the snare laid for man's destruction with a fair pretence of love to advance man to a greater happiness, and so pretendeth the good of those whom he meaneth wholly to destroy. He enticeth the covetous with dishonest gain, which at length proveth a real loss; the sensual with vain pleasures, which at length prove the greatest pain to body and soul: the ambitious with honours, which really tend to their disgrace. Always trust God, but disbelieve the devil, who promoteth man's destruction under a pretence of his good and happiness. How can Satan and his instruments put us upon [promote] anything that is really good for us?

Fourthly, *that Satan's first temptations are more plausible.* He doth not at first dash [approach] come with 'fall down and worship me'; but only pretendeth a respect to Christ's refection [refreshment], and a demonstration of his sonship. Few or none are so desperate at first as to leap into hell at the first dash, therefore the devil beginneth with the least temptations. First, men begin with less evils, play about the brink of hell: a man at first taketh a liking to [evil] company, afterwards he doth a little enlarge himself into some haunts and merry meetings with his companions, then entereth into a confederacy in evil, till he hath brought utter ruin upon himself, and what was honest friendship at first proveth wicked company and sure destruction at last. At first a man playeth [gambles] for recreation, then ventureth a shilling or two [i.e. a small sum of money], afterwards, by the witchery [addiction] of gaming, off goeth all sense of thrift, honesty and credit. At first a man dispenseth [compromises] with himself in some duty, then his dispensation [compromise] groweth into a settled toleration, and God is cast out of his closet [i.e. he stops praying in secret], and his heart groweth dead, dry and sapless. There is no stop [limit] in sin, it is of a multiplying nature, and we go on from one degree to another; and a little lust sets open the door for a greater, as the lesser [smaller] sticks set the greater on fire.

Fifthly, *there is no way to defeat Satan's temptation but by a sound belief of God's all-sufficiency, and the nothingless of the creature.*

(1) A sound belief of, and a dependence on, God's all-sufficiency: 'I am the Almighty God; walk before me, and be thou perfect' (Genesis 17:1). We need not warp [do evil], nor run to our shifts [expedients]; he is enough to help to defend or reward us; he can help us without means, though there be no supply in the view of sense or full heaps in our own keeping. God knoweth when we know not: 'The Lord knoweth how to deliver the godly out of temptations ...'(2 Peter 2:9), or by contrary means, curing the eyes with spittle and clay. He can make a little means go far. As he blessed the pulse to the captive children (Daniel 1:15), and made the widow's barrel of meal and cruse of oil to hold out (1 Kings 17:14), and his filling and feeding five thousand with a few barley loaves and a few fishes (Matthew 14:21). On the other side he can make abundance unprofitable: 'A man's life consisteth not in the abundance of the things which he possesseth' (Luke 12:15). No means can avail unless God giveth his blessing; therefore we should not distrust his providence, nor attempt anything without God's warrant, lest we offend him, and provoke him to withdraw his blessing.

(2) The nothingness of the creature: 'Not by bread alone'. It is nothing by way of comparison with God, nothing by

way of exclusion of God, nothing in opposition to God. It should be nothing in our esteem, so far as it would be something separate from God, or in co-ordination with God: 'All nations before him are as nothing, less than nothing and vanity' (Isaiah 40:17); 'Now ye are nothing' (Job 6:21). All friends cannot help, our foes cannot hurt us, not the greatest of either kind [friends and enemies]: 'All her princes shall be nothing' (Isaiah 34:12). In regard of the effects which the world promiseth to its deluded lovers, all is as nothing; not only that it can do nothing to our needy souls to relieve us from the burden of sin, nothing towards the quiet and true peace of our wounded consciences, nothing to our acceptance with God, nothing for strength against corruptions and temptations, nothing at the hour of death; but it can do nothing for us during life, nothing to relieve and satisfy us in the world without God. Therefore God is still [at all times] to be owned [confessed] and trusted.

3

Then the devil taketh him up into the holy city, and setteth him on a pinnacle of the temple, and saith unto him, If thou be the Son of God, cast thyself down: for it is written, He shall give his angels charge concerning thee; and in their hands they shall bear thee up, lest at any time thou dash thy foot against a stone (Matthew 4:5, 6).

In this second temptation I shall give you: (1) the history of it; (2) observations upon it.

1. The history of it. There (1) what Satan did; (2) what he said; (3) the soreness of the temptation.

1. What he did: 'Then the devil taketh him up into the holy city, and setteth him on a pinnacle of the temple'.

There: (1) Take notice of the ground which the devil chose for the conflict: 'He taketh him up into the holy city, and setteth him on the pinnacle of the temple.' By the *holy city* is meant Jerusalem, for this name is given to it in other scriptures: 'They call themselves of the holy city' (Isaiah 58:2); and 'O Jerusalem, the holy city' (Isaiah 52:1); and in many other places. It was so called, because it was the seat of God's worship, and the place where God manifested his gracious presence with his people. If you ask why now it was called the holy city, since it was a city of blood, the seat of all wickedness, in which the law of God was depraved, their religion corrupted, their religion polluted? I answer, Yet there was the temple of the Lord. Some relics of good and holy men, some grace yet continued, and the only place that owned the true God, though with much corruption. The more especial place which the devil chose for the conflict was *pterygion tou hierou*, 'the pinnacle of the temple', or 'the wing of the temple'; meaning the border round about the flat covering of the temple to hinder any one from falling off easily, which might be adorned with pinnacles and spires, from whence one might easily fall.

(2) How the devil got him there. Was Christ carried through the air or did he go on his feet, following him of his own accord? The last seemeth to be countenanced [suggested] by Luke; that he led him to the pinnacle of the temple (Luke 4:9, [*egagen auton*: he led him]); yet the former is preferred by most ancient and modern interpreters, and not without reason. For Christ voluntarily to follow the devil, and to go up to the top of the temple, and stand on one of the pinnacles thereof, it seemeth improbable and would take up more time than could be spent on this temptation. He that would not obey the devil persuading him to cast himself down, that he might not tempt God, would not voluntarily have gone up with him, for that would have been the beginning of a temptation, to yield so far. Most probably, then, Satan was permitted to carry him in the air, without doing him any hurt, to Jerusalem, and one of the pinnacles of the temple and battlements thereof. But how Christ was carried in the air, visibly or invisibly, the scripture showeth not: it affirmeth the thing, but sets not down the manner. We must believe what it asserteth, [and] reverence [respect] what it concealeth. Here was a real translation, a transportation from place to place, not imaginary, for then Christ had been in no danger. And again, not violent, but voluntary – a carrying, not a haling [dragging forcibly] – a leading, not

a forcing, as the wrestler is drawn on to the combat. As he suffered [permitted] himself to be drawn to death by Satan's instruments, so [he allows himself] by the devil to be translated from place to place.

The officers of the high priest had power to carry him from the garden to Annas, from Annas to Caiaphas, from Caiaphas to Pilate, from Pilate to Herod, from Herod to Pilate again, and then from Gabbatha to Golgotha, which could not have been unless this power had been given them from above, as Christ himself telleth Pilate (John 19:11). So God, for his greater glory and our instruction, permitted this transportation. Therefore this translation is not to be imputed to the weakness of Christ, but his patience, submitting thus far that he might experience all the machinations [crafty tricks] of Satan. And the transporting is not to be ascribed to the tempter's strength, but [to] his boldness. Christ did not obey him, but submitted to the divine dispensation, and would fight with him not only in the desert, but in the holy city: and no wonder if Christ suffered Satan to carry him, who [since Christ] suffered his instruments [sinners] to crucify him.

2. What he said to him (verse 6), where take notice: (1) Of the temptation itself, 'If thou be the Son of God, cast thyself down.'; (2) The reason alleged to back it, 'For it is written, He shall give his angels charge concerning thee', etc.

(1) *The temptation itself*: 'If thou be the Son of God, cast thyself down.'

Mark [notice] what was the mote [object] in the devil's eye [mind]: that Christ was declared to be the Son of God, the Messiah and Saviour of the world. He would have him to put it to this proof in the sight of all Jerusalem. Wherein [in this], if he had failed, and had died of the fall, the Jews would think him an imposter. If he had escaped, he had [would have] submitted to the devil's methods, and so had [would have] run into the former sins mentioned before in the first temptation, namely his doing something at the devil's direction. His disbelief of the divine oracle, unless manifested by such proof as Satan required; and besides a tempting of divine providence – the ordinary way was down stairs. He would have him leap, and throw himself over the battlements. It would be too long to go downstairs; he will teach him a nearer way: to cast himself down and fear no hurt, for if he were the Son of God he might securely do so. But chiefly Christ was not to begin his ministry by miracles, but doctrine – not from a demonstration of his power, but wisdom. The gospel was to be first preached, then sealed and confirmed by miracles; and Christ's miracles were not to be ludicrous, but profitable – not fitted for pomp, but use – to instruct and help men, rather than strike them with wonder. Now this would discredit the gospel, if Christ should fly in the air; besides, we must not fly to extraordinary means [of help], where ordinary are present.

Only, before I go off [leave this point], observe that Satan did not offer to cast him down. That God did not suffer him to do, because he sought to bring Christ to sin. If Satan had cast him down, Christ had [would not have] not sinned.

(2) *The reason by which he backeth the temptation.*
It is taken from scripture: 'For it is written, He shall give his angels charge concerning thee.' The scripture is in Psalm 91:11, 12, where the words run thus: 'He shall give his angels charge over thee, to keep thee in all thy ways. They

shall bear thee up in their hands, lest thou dash thy foot against a stone.' Where,

First, *observe the devil's cunning in citing scripture.* The apostle telleth us that Satan is sometimes transformed into an angel of light (2 Corinthians 11:14). And we read that once he took the habit and guise of a prophet (1 Samuel 28:18); and indeed he deceiveth more by the voice of Samuel than by the voice of the dragon. We read of *ta bathe tou Satana,* 'The depths of Satan' (Revelation 2:24). Here he cometh like a divine, with a Bible in his hand, and turneth to the place [in the Bible]; here the enemy of God cometh with the Word of God, and disguiseth the worst of actions with the best of words, opposeth God to God, and turneth his truth to countenance a lie. Being refuted by scripture, he will bring scripture too, and pretendeth to reverence that which he chiefly hateth. Christians, you have not to do with a foolish devil, who will appear in his own colours and ugly shape, but with a devout devil, who, for his own turn [for his own purposes], can pretend to be godly.

Secondly, *that he citeth such a scripture*, which exceedingly conduceth [tends] to commend the happiness of the godly; for God will not only be the keeper and guardian of them that fear him, but hath also appointed the ministry of angels; and the argument of the tempter seemeth to be taken from the less to the greater; for if it be true of every one that trusts in God, and dwelleth in the shadow of the Almighty, that God will have such a care of him, much more will he have a care of his beloved Son, in whom he is well pleased. Therefore, [argues Satan], you that are declared to be so from heaven, and having such an occasion to show yourself to be the Son of God with so much honour and profit, why should you scruple to cast yourself down?

But wherein was the devil faulty in citing the scripture? Some say in leaving out those words, *in all thy ways*. This was Bernard's gloss [comment]: *in viis, non in praecipitiis* [in your ways, not in your reckless actions]: will keep you in your ways of duties, not in your headlong actions; these were none of his ways, to throw himself down from the battlements of the temple. This [comment] is not to be altogether rejected, because it reaches the sense. Yet this omission was not the devil's fault in citing this scripture; for, *all thy ways* signifieth no more but [than] in all thy actions and businesses, and that is sufficiently implied in the words cited by Satan. But the devil's error was in application. He applieth the word of God, not to instruct, but deceive; rather to breed a contempt, disdain, and hatred of scriptures, than a reverent esteem of them; to make the Word of God seem uncertain; or if a reverence of them, to turn this reverence into an occasion of deceit; more particularly to tempt God to a needless proof of his power. We are not to cast ourselves into danger, that providence may fetch [rescue] us off. God will protect us in the evils we suffer, not in the evils we commit; not in dangers we seek, but such as befall us besides our intention.

3. The soreness of this temptation, which appeareth in several things.

1. *The change of place*
For a new temptation, he maketh choice of a new place; he could do no good on him in the wilderness, therefore he taketh him and carrieth him into the holy city. Here was a public place where Christ might discover himself with profit, and the edification of many, if he would but submit

to the devil's methods. In the temple the Messiah was as in his own house, where it was fit the Messiah should exhibit himself to his people. There was an old prophecy 'The Lord, whom ye seek, shall suddenly come into his temple, even the messenger of the covenant, whom ye delight in' (Malachi 3:1). And he was to send forth his rod out of Zion, even the law of his kingdom (Psalm 110:2). If he would yield to this advice and vain-glorious ostentation [display] of his power before that numerous multitude which continually resorted to the holy things performed in the temple, how soon should he be manifested to the Son of God, or the power of the great God! The devil doth not persuade him to cast himself from a rock or top of a tree in the desert – that had [would have] been temerity and rashness – but from a pinnacle of the temple, an holy place, and a place of much resort. But the Son of God was not to be discovered to the world by the devil's methods. That had [would have] been such a piece of ostentation and vainglory as did not become the Son of God, who came to teach the world humility. But, however, the temptation is grievous: in so good a design, in such an holy place, there could no ill happen to the Son of God, nor a better occasion be offered of showing himself to many, so to confirm the Jews in the truth of the oracle [which] they had of late heard from heaven.

2. *The change of temptations*

Since he [Christ] will trust [in God], the devil will put him upon [encourage] trusting; he shall trust as much as he will. There he tempted him to the use of unlawful means to preserve his life, here to the neglect of things lawful. There, [Satan tempted Christ to suppose] that God would fail him if he were still obedient to the Spirit, and did not take another course [of action] than divine providence had as yet offered to him. Here, [Satan tempts Christ to think] that God would not forsake him though he threw himself into danger. There, that he would fail though he had promised; here, that he would help though he had not promised. That faith which sustained him in his hunger would preserve him in this precipice [the throwing himself down]; if he expected his preservation from God, why not now? He had hitherto tempted him to diffidence, now to prefidence [presumption], or an over-confident presumption that God would needlessly show his power. It is usual with the tempter to tempt man on both sides; sometimes to weaken his faith, at other times to neglect his duty. He was cast out of heaven himself, and he is all for casting down.

3. *The temptation was the more strong, being veiled under a pretence of scripture,* and so Christ's weapons seem to be beaten back upon himself. The devil tempted him to nothing but what he might be confident to do upon the promise of God. Now it is grievous to God's children, when the rule of their lives and the charter of their hopes [the Bible and its promises] is abused to countenance a temptation.

Observations

(1) Observe, *that the first temptation being rejected by Christ, Satan maketh a new assault.* Though he get the foil [is thwarted], he will set on us again; like a troublesome fly that is often beaten off, yet will return to the same place. Thus the devil, when he could do no good upon his first patent [licence to tempt] against Job's goods and children, cometh and sueth [asked God] for a new commission, that he might touch his flesh and bones: 'Skin for skin, yea, all that a man hath will he give for his life. But put forth thine

hand now, and touch his bone and his flesh, and he will curse thee to thy face (Job 2:4, 5). Satan is incessant in his attempts against the saints, and is ready to assault afresh upon every occasion. Now this cometh to pass by [because of] Satan's unwearied malice, who is a sworn enemy to our peace and welfare – he still 'seeketh to devour' us (1 Peter 5:8); also from God's providence, who permitteth this that we may not be careless and secure after temptation, though we have gotten the victory. For our life is a continual warfare: 'Is there not an appointed time for man upon earth?' (Job 7:1). The same word signifieth also a warfare.

Man's life is a perpetual toil, and a condition of manifold temptations and hazards, such as a soldier is exposed to; therefore we must perpetually watch. We get not an absolute victory till death. Now this should the more prevail with us, because many of God's people have failed after some eminent service performed for God. Josiah, after he had prepared the temple, fell into that rash attempt against Pharaoh Necho which cost him his life: 'After all this, when Josiah had prepared the temple, Necho, king of Egypt, came up to fight against Carchemish by Euphrates; and Josiah went out against him' (2 Chronicles 35:20). And Peter, after he had made a glorious confession, giveth his Master carnal counsel: 'Thou art Peter, and upon this rock will I build my church ...' (Matthew 16:18) and yet, 'Get thee behind me, Satan' (verse 23). Many, after they have been much lifted up in consolation, do readily miscarry [go astray]. First, he made a glorious confession, a sign of great faith; then carnal wisdom vents itself [is spoken by him] in some counsel concerning the ease of the flesh. Oh, what need have we to stand upon our guard, till God tread Satan under our feet! As one of the Roman generals, whether conquering or conquered, *semper instaurat pugnam* [always renews the fight], so doth Satan.

(2) Observe, *God may give Satan some power over the body of one whom he loveth dearly*. For Satan is permitted to transport Christ's body from the wilderness to the holy city, as to set it on a pinnacle of the temple. As it is very consistent with God's love to his people to suffer them to be tempted in their souls by the fiery darts of Satan, so he may permit Satan to afflict their bodies, either by himself, or by witches, who are his instruments. Thus he permitted Satan to afflict Job: 'And the LORD said unto Satan, Behold he is in thy hand, but save his life. So went Satan forth from the presence of the LORD, and smote Job with sore boils, from the sole of his foot unto his crown' (Job 2:6, 7). The devil may have a threefold power over the bodies of men:

(i) By transportations, or carrying them from one place to another, which usually is not found but in those that give up themselves to his diabolical enchantments. Or:

(ii) In possessions, which were frequent, and rife in Christ's time: 'My daughter is sorely vexed with a devil' (Matthew 15:22). Or:

(iii) In diseases, which is more common. Thus he afflicted Job's body with ulcers; and what we read, 'An evil disease cleaveth fast unto him' (Psalm 41:8). It is *debharbelial,* 'a thing of Belial', as if it were a pestilential disease from the devil. So some understand that: 'Surely he shall deliver thee from the snare of the fowler, and from the noisome pestilence' (Psalm 91:3). As if those sudden darts of venom by which we are stricken in the plague came from Satan. Certainly evil angels may have a great hand in our diseases: 'He cast upon them the fierceness of his anger, wrath, and indignation, and trouble, by sending evil angels among them' (Psalm 78:49). But I press it not much [I do not want to overstrain this argument]. Only:

(a) *A word of patience*, that we would submit to God, though our trials be never so sharp. We must yield to that measure of humiliation which it shall please God to prescribe. If he should give leave to Satan to inflame our blood and trouble the humours [physical conditions thought to affect our moods] of our body, we must not repine [complain]; the Son of God permitted his sacred body to be transported by the devil in the air.

(b) *A word of comfort*. Whatever power God permitteth Satan to have over our bodies, or bodily interests, yet it is limited; he cannot hurt or molest any further than God pleaseth. He had power to set Christ on a pinnacle of the temple, but not to cast him down. He had a power to touch Job's skin, but a charge not to endanger his life: 'Behold, he is in thine hand, but save his life' (Job 2:6). God sets bounds and limits to the malice of Satan, that he is not able to compass [achieve] all his designs [plans]. Job was to be exercised, but God would not have him die in a cloud [in obscurity]; his life was to be secured till better times.

(c) *A word of caution*. Let not the devil make [take] an advantage of those troubles which he bringeth upon our bodies, or the interests of the bodily life, yet let him not thereby draw you to sin. Here the devil may set Christ upon a precipice, but he can do him no further hurt; he may persuade us to cast down ourselves, but he cannot cast us down unless we cast down ourselves, *Nemo laeditur nisi a seipso* [no one is hurt but the person who hurts himself]. His main spite is at your souls, to involve you in sin. God may give him and his instruments a power over your bodily lives, but he doth not give him a power over the graces of the saints. The devil aimeth at the destruction of souls; he can let men enjoy the pleasures of sin for a season, that he may deprive you of delight in God and celestial pleasures. He can be content that you shall have dignities and honours if they prove a snare to you. If the devil seek to bring you to poverty, trouble, and nakedness, it is to draw you from God. He careth not for the body but as it may be an occasion to ruin the soul.

(3) Observe, *if Satan lead us up, it is to throw us down.* He taketh up Christ to the pinnacle of the temple, and saith unto him, 'Cast thyself down'. He bringeth up [honours] many [people] by little and little to some high place [place of honour], that by their aspiring they may at length break their necks [i.e. go into hell]. Thus he did Haman, and so he doth many others, whose climbing maketh way for their greater fall. The devil himself was an aspirer, and fell from heaven like lightning: 'I beheld Satan as lightning fall from heaven' (Luke 10:18). And though in show he may seem to befriend many that hearken to his temptations, yet in the end he crieth, 'Down with them, down with them, even to the ground.' God's manner is quite contrary; when he meaneth to exalt a man, he will first humble him, and make him low: 'Whosoever shall exalt himself shall be abased; and he that shall humble himself shall be exalted' (Matthew 22:12). But the devil's way is to lift them up to the clouds, that he may bring them down to the lowest pit of destruction. Adam, in conceit, must be [attempted to be] like God, that indeed he may [through the punishment of death] be like the beasts that perish: 'Man that is in honour, and understandeth not, is like the beasts that perish' (Psalm 49:20).

(4) Observe, 'If thou be the Son of God, cast thyself down'; *the temptation is quite contrary to what it was before*. Then it was to preserve life by unlawful means, now to endanger life by the neglect of means lawful; there to distrust God's care of our preservation when he hath set us about any task or work, here to presume on his care without warrant. The devil tempts us sometimes to pamper the flesh, sometimes to neglect it in such a way as is destructive to our service. Thus the devil hurrieth us from one extreme to another, as the possessed man 'fell oft-times into the fire, and oft into the water' (Matthew 17:15). Those that are guided by Satan reel from one extremity to another; either men slight sin and make light of it, or sinners are apt to sorrow above measure, as the incestuous Corinthian: 'Lest perhaps such an one should be swallowed up with overmuch sorrow' (2 Corinthians 2:17). And the apostle showeth there that these were the enterprises of Satan.

Some men are careless of God's interest in the world, or else heated into the activity of a bitter zeal. Some are of a scrupulous spirit, that they may make conscience of all things; and the devil hurrieth them into a large [liberal and] atheistical spirit, that they make conscience of nothing. How often have we known a fond [foolish] scrupulosity [over-scrupulousness] to end in profane licentiousness, when they have been wearied out of that kind of frame of spirit! Some are dead and heartless. Like Gallio, they 'care for none of these'. [They] fight Christ, [and they] fight Antichrist; it is all one to them. And usually they are such as formerly have been heated with a blind and bold madness, as Peter [who] at first refused to have his feet washed by Christ, and then would have head, hands, feet and all washed (John 13:8, 9), being out in both [he went too far].

What sad work is there made in the church of God by Solifidians and Nullifidians.[6] Heretofore it was all faith and free grace misapplied and misunderstood; and now it is all morality and virtue, while Christ is neglected, and the mystery of the gospel little set by or valued. It is ever the devil's policy to work upon the humour of people. If they will reform the church, it shall be to a degree of separation, and condemning all churches and Christians that are not of their mode; if they be for uniting, Christ's unquestionable interests must be trodden underfoot, and all care of truth and reformation must be laid aside. If he can destroy religion and godliness [in] no other way, he will be religious and godly himself; but it is either, as to private Christians, to set them upon overdoing, that he may make them weary of the service of Christ; or, as to the public, by crying up [overpraising] some unnecessary things which Christ never commanded. If men be troubled with sin, and see a necessity of the gospel, and prize the comforts of it, the gospel must be 'over-gospelled', or else it will not serve their turns. And that 'over-gospel' must be carried to such a length as to destroy the very gospel, and free grace itself. The devil first tempted the world to despise the poor fishermen that preached the gospel; but the world, being convinced by the power of the Holy Ghost, and gained to the faith, then he [Satan] fought by riches and grandeur to debase the gospel; so that he hath got as much, or more, by the worldly glory he puts upon Christ's messengers as by persecution. Then when that is discovered [seen to be corrupt], the devil will turn 'reformer'; and what 'reformation' is that? The very neces-

---

6. Solifidians: those who press 'faith alone' too far; Nullifidians: those who deny faith.

SERMON 3   71

sary support and maintenance of ministers must be taken away! All overdoing in God's work is undoing. If Christ will trust, the devil will persuade him to trust, even to the degree of tempting God.

(5) Observe, *that the devil himself may pretend [to believe] scripture [so as] to put a varnish upon his [own] evil designs*; for here he seeketh to foil Christ with his [Christ's] own weapons: which serveth to prevent a double extreme [keep us from going to either extreme in life].

(i) One is, not to be frighted with the mere noise and sound of scriptures, which men bring to countenance their errors. See whether they be not wrested and misapplied; for the devil may quote scripture, but he perverts the meaning of it. And usually it is so by his instruments; as that pope, who would prove a double power to be in himself, temporal and spiritual, by that scripture, *Ecce duo gladii!* 'Behold, here are two swords!' (Luke 22:38). It is easy to rehearse the words of scripture, and therefore not the bare words, but the *meaning* must be regarded [attended to].

(ii) The other extreme is this: Let none vilify [think low thoughts of] the scriptures, because pleaded by Satan; for so he might as well vilify human reason, which is pleaded for all the errors in the world; or law, because it is urged sometimes to justify a bad cause. For it is not scripture, that is a nose of wax [can prove anything you like], as Papists say. It is a great proof of the authority and honour of scriptures, that Satan and his greatest instruments do place their greatest hopes of prevailing by perverting and misapplying of it.

(6) Observe, That God hath given his angels a special charge about his people, to keep them from harm. Here I shall show: (a) that it is so; (b) why it is so.

First, *that it is so is evident by the scripture*, which everywhere shows us that angels are the first instruments of his providence, which he maketh use of in guarding his faithful servants (Hebrews 1:14). The apostle saith, 'Are they not all *leitourgika pneumata* [ministering spirits], sent forth to minister to them that shall be the heirs of salvation?' Their work and employment is to attend us at God's direction, not to be worshipped and served by us by any devotion. They are 'ministering spirits', not ours but Christ's; he that serveth hath a master whom he serveth, and by whom he is sent forth. Their work and employment is to attend us indeed, but at the command and direction of their own Master. They are not at our beck [and call] to go and come at our pleasure, neither do they go and come at their [own] inclination, but at the commission of God. Their work is appointed by him; they serve us as their Master's children, at his command and will. And whom do they serve? 'The heirs of salvation'. They [these 'heirs'] are described, 'That being justified by grace, we should be made heirs according to the hope of eternal life' (Titus 3:7). They [the angels] are not ministers of conversion and sanctification; to this ministry Christ hath called *men*, not angels; but in preserving the converted the angels have a hand. Therefore it is notable they are sometimes called 'God's angels': 'Bless the LORD, all ye his hosts, ye ministers of his that do his pleasure' (Psalm 103:21); sometimes 'their angels': 'Take heed that ye despise not one of these little ones, for I say unto you, that in heaven their angels do always behold the face of my Father which is in heaven' (Matthew 17:10).

But whether every one hath a guardian-angel is a curious question. Sometimes one angel serveth many persons: 'The angel of the LORD encampeth round about them that fear him, and delivereth them' (Psalm 34:7), and sometimes many angels are about one person: 'And, behold, the mountain was full of horses and chariots round about Elisha' (2 Kings 6:17). And here in the text quoted by Satan, 'He shall give his angels charge concerning thee.' There is not mention made of one, but [of] many angels; and the angels in general are said to be 'ministering spirits'. When soldiers are said to watch for a city, it is not meant that every citizen hath a soldier to watch for him.

The only place which seemeth to countenance that opinion is Acts 12:15: 'Then said they, It is his angel.' But if Peter had a peculiar angel to guard him, and look after him then, when he was in great trouble, and detained in prison, it doth not follow that every person and everywhere should have a guardian-angel. Besides, an assertion in scripture must be distinguished from men introduced speaking [persons speaking incorrectly] in scripture. It showeth, indeed, that it was the opinion of the Jews at that time, which these holy men had imbibed and drunk in. Or it may be the word *angel* is only taken for a *messenger* sent from Peter. Why should an angel stand knocking at the door, who could easily make his entrance? And is it credible that the guardian angels do take the shape and habit [clothing of those people] whose angels they are? It is enough for us to believe that all the angels are our guardians, who are sent to keep us and preserve us, as it pleaseth God.

But what is their ministry and custody? It is not *cura animarum* [the care of souls], care and charge of souls; that Christ taketh upon himself, and performeth it by his Spirit;

but *ministerium externi auxilii* [the ministry of external help], to afford us outward help and relief; it is *custodia carporis* [protection of the body], they guard the bodily life chiefly. Thus we find them often employed. An angel brought Elijah his food under the juniper-tree (1 Kings 19:5). An angel stirred the water at the Pool of Siloam (John 5:40). An angel was the guide of the way to Abraham's servant: 'He will send his angel before thee, and thou shalt take a wife unto my son from thence' (Genesis 24:7). Angels defend us against enemies: 'The angel of the LORD encampeth round about them that fear him, and delivereth them' (Psalm 34:7); 'The angel of the LORD went out, and smote in the camp of the Assyrians an hundred fourscore and five thousand' (2 Kings 19:35). An angel opened the prison doors to the apostles: (Acts 5:19 and 12:7).

But were not all these services extraordinary and miraculous, which we may not now expect? *Answer*. The visible ministry was extraordinary, proper to those times; but the invisible is perpetual and ordinary, as Abraham's servant did not see the angel in the journey. The devil worketh in and about wicked men invisibly; so do the good angels.

Secondly, Reasons why it is so.

(1) To manifest the great love and care which God hath over his people; therefore he giveth those blessed spirits, which behold his face, charge concerning his people on earth; as if a nobleman were charged [commanded] to look to a beggar by the prince of both [by the prince who ruled over them both].

(2) We understand the operation of finite agents better than infinite. God is so far out of the reach of our commerce [experience], that we cannot understand the particularity of his providence.

(3) To counterwork [frustrate] the devil: evil angels are ready to hurt us, and therefore good angels are ready to preserve us. Well might the devil be so well versed in this place [of Scripture quoted by him here]. He hath often felt the effects of it; he knew it by experience, being so often encountered by the good angels in his endeavours against the people of God.

(4) To begin our acquaintance, which in heaven shall be perfected: 'Ye are come to an innumerable company of angels' (Hebrews 12:22).

Uses

Use 1: *To show the happy state of God's people.* No heirs of a crown have such guards as they have. Christ dwelleth in their hearts as in a throne: 'That Christ may dwell in your hearts by faith' (Ephesians 3:17). The Holy Spirit guardeth them against all cares and fears: 'And the peace of God, which passeth all understanding, shall keep your hearts and minds through Jesus Christ' (Philippians 4:7). And the good angels are as a wall and camp about them: 'The angel of the LORD encampeth round about them that fear him, and delivereth them' (Psalm 34:7); 'Despise not one of these little ones, for verily I say unto you, that in heaven their angels do always behold the face of my Father which is in heaven' (Matthew 17:10). If the angels make an account of them, surely men should not despise them; yea, rather, God esteemeth so much of the meanest of these little ones, that the good angels, who daily enjoy God's glorious presence, are ministering spirits appointed to attend them. If the Lord and his holy angels set such a price on the meanest Christians, we should be loth to despise and offend them.

Use 2: *It should breed some confidence and comfort in Christians in their sore straits and difficulties, when all visible help seemeth to be cut off.* This invisible ministry of the angels is matter of faith: 'And he answered, Fear not: for they that be with us are more than they that be with them. And Elisha prayed, and said, LORD, I pray thee, open the young man's eyes, that he may see. And the LORD opened the young man's eyes, and he saw: and, behold, the mountain was full of horses and chariots of fire round about Elisha' (2 Kings 6:16, 17). These were no other but the angels of God, which were as an host to defend them. Open the eye of faith, [that] you may see God and his holy angels to secure you.

Use 3: *Take we heed [let us take heed] how we carry ourselves [behave], because of this honourable presence.* In congregations there should be no indecency, 'because of the angels' (1 Corinthians 11:10). In all our ways let us take heed that we do not step out of God's way. Do nothing that is unseemly and dishonest; they [the angels] are spies upon us [they are watching us in our church worship]. And it is profitable for us, that they may give an account of us to God with joy, and not with grief.

4

*Jesus said unto him, It is written again,
Thou shalt not tempt the Lord thy God*
(Matthew 4:7).

Here is Christ's answer to the second temptation, where two things are observable: first, that Christ answered; secondly, what he answered.

First, That Christ answered

Christ answered, the more to convince and confound this old deceiver, that he might not think that he was ignorant of his sleights [tricks], or that he fainted in the conflict; as also to instruct us what to do in the renewed assaults of the devil, to keep up our resistance still, letting go [keeping firm to] our sure hold, which are the scriptures.

Secondly, What he answered

'It is written', etc. But would it not have been more satisfactory to have said, It is sufficiently manifest to me that I am the Son of God, and cared for by him, and that it is not for the children of God to run upon precipices?

I answer: It is not for human wisdom to interpose and prescribe to Christ, who was the wisdom and power of God. His answer is most satisfactory, for two reasons: (1) It striketh at the throat of the cause; (2) It doth with advantage give us other instructions.

(1) Christ cutteth the throat of the temptation by quoting a passage of scripture, out of Deuteronomy 6:16, 'Ye shall

not tempt the LORD your God, as ye tempted him in Massah.' If we must not tempt God, then it doth not become Christ to tempt his Father's providence for a new proof of his filiation[7] and care over him. Therefore the devil's temptation was neither good nor profitable, to put either his sonship or the care of God's providence to this trial; as if he had said, I shall not require any more signs to prove my filiation, nor express any doubt of his power and goodness towards me, as the Israelites did: 'And he called the name of the place Massah, and Meribah, because of the chiding of the children of Israel, and because they tempted the LORD, saying, Is the LORD among us, or not?' (Exodus 17:7). To which story this prohibition of tempting God alludeth.

(2) He doth with advantage give us other instructions; as, (i) That we must not esteem the less of scripture, though Satan and his instruments abuse it; and that nothing is more profitable to dissolve doubts and objections raised from scripture, than to compare one scripture with another. For scripture is not opposite to scripture. There is a fair agreement and harmony between the truths therein compared; and one place doth not cross [contradict] another, but clear and explain [elucidate] another. One place saith he hath a great care of his people, and useth the ministry of angels for that end and purpose; but another place saith, 'Thou shalt not tempt the Lord thy God'; they must not seek out dangers, and forfeit their protection by unreasonable presumption.

(ii) It teacheth us that what the scripture speaketh to all, is to be esteemed as spoken to every singular person, for they are included in their universality. In Deuteronomy it is,

---

7. 'Filiation': see note, p.51

'Ye shall not tempt the Lord *your* God'; but Christ accommodateth it to his own purpose, 'Thou shalt not tempt the Lord *thy* God'. He that is not to be tempted by a multitude, is not to be tempted by any one. So Psalm 27:8, 'When thou saidst, Seek ye my face, my heart said unto thee, Thy face, LORD, will I seek.' God's words invite all, but David maketh application to himself.

(3) Christ subjects himself to the moral law[8], and did apply the precepts thereof to himself, no less than to us; and so is a pattern of obedience to us, that we ought to direct and order all our actions according to the law and word of God.

Doctrine: Tempting [of] God may be a usual [common], but yet it is a great and heinous sin. In speaking to this point, I shall show: (1) What this tempting of God is; (2) The heinousness of the sin.

I. What is this tempting of God? And here let me speak: (1) To the object; (2) To the act.

1. The object, *The Lord thy God.*
To us Christians there is but one only true God – Father, Son and Holy Ghost. Now sometimes we are said to tempt God, and sometimes Christ, and sometimes the Spirit of God.

(1) In scripture we are said to tempt God, as in Psalm 95:9: 'When you fathers tempted me, proved me, and saw my works.' We tempt God either explicitly or implicitly.

(i) Explicitly, by plain and direct words, which tend to

---

8. The moral law: the Ten Commandments, which are a rule of life to Christians, though they cannot save us.

God's dishonour; or a doubting of his prescience [foreknowledge], power and providence, if they have not all things given them according to their fancies and humours [wishes]. As Psalm 78:18, 19, 'They tempted God in their hearts, by asking meat for their lusts. Yea, they spake against God, and said, Can God provide a table in the wilderness?' So Exodus 17:7, 'Is the LORD in the midst of us, or no?' They doubted whether God's presence were among them, when they had continually such pregnant [clearest] proofs of it. The words may either bear this sense, Who knows that God is present? or, Now see whether God be present, or takes any care of us, yea or no.

(ii) Implicitly, or by interpretation, which is a more secret way of tempting God, when the act speaketh [implies] it, whatever be the intention of the doer. As those who were about to lay the burden of the rites of Moses' law on the new converts of the Gentiles: 'Now, therefore, why tempt ye God, to put a yoke upon the necks of the disciples, which neither our fathers nor we were able to bear?' (Acts 15:10). That is, why do you not acquiesce in the will of God, apparently manifested, as if ye did go about to try whether God did require anything of his servants besides faith in Christ? His will was clearly evident in the case by what happened to Cornelius; or as if ye would try whether God will take it well that ye should impose upon his disciples a yoke that he approveth not.

(2) We are said to tempt Christ; and he may be considered either as in the days of his flesh, or in his state of glory, and with respect to his invisible presence:

(i) In the days of his flesh he was frequently tempted by the scribes and Pharisees, who would not be satisfied in his

SERMON 4   81

mission, notwithstanding all the signs and wonders that he had wrought among them; or else sought to accuse and disgrace him, and prejudice the people against him; so Matthew 16:1, 'The Pharisees with the Sadducees came, and tempting him, desired him that he would show them a sign from heaven.' So Matthew 22:18, 'Why tempt ye me, ye hypocrites?' when the Pharisees and the Herodians came to question him about paying tribute. So Luke 10:25, 'A certain lawyer stood up, and tempted him', etc.

(ii) In his state of glory, and with respect to his invisible presence. So the Israelites in the wilderness tempted him before his coming in the flesh, and Christians may now tempt him after his ascension into heaven. Both are in one place: 'Neither let us tempt Christ, as some of them also tempted, and were destroyed of serpents' (1 Corinthians 10:9). What was their tempting of Christ in the wilderness?

If he be considered as God, he had a subsistence before he was incarnate of the Virgin; and in this sense, as they tempted God, so they may be said also to tempt Christ; for all the affliction, shame, and disgrace done to that people are called the reproach of Christ: 'Choosing rather to suffer affliction with the people of God, than to enjoy the pleasures of sin for a season; esteeming the reproach of Christ greater riches than the treasures of Egypt' (Hebrews 11:25, 26). So their murmuring might be called a tempting of Christ.

Christ was the perpetual head of the church, who in his own person did lead the people, and was present in the midst of them under the notion [concept] of the angel of the covenant. The eternal Son of God guided them in the wilderness: 'Behold, I will send an angel before thee, to keep thee in the way, and to bring thee into the place which I have prepared. Beware of him, and obey his voice, provoke him not; for he will not pardon your transgressions; for my name is in him. But if thou shalt indeed obey his voice, and do all that I speak, then I will be an enemy to thy enemies, and an adversary unto thy adversaries; for mine angel shall go before thee, and bring thee in unto the land of the Amorites ...' (Exodus 23:20-23). This angel can be no other than Christ, whose office it is to keep us in the way, and to bring us into the place which Christ hath prepared for us; he it is that must be obeyed by the people of God, and pardon their transgressions; in him is God's name, for he will not communicate it to any other that is not of the same substance with himself: God is in him, and he in the Father, and his name is 'Jehovah our Righteousness'. So Exodus 33:14, 'My presence shall go with thee, and I will give thee rest.' My presence, that is, my angel, spoken of before, called 'the angel of his presence'. 'In all their affliction he was afflicted, and the angel of his presence saved them' (Isaiah 63:9). This angel is called Jehovah in Exodus 13:21: 'And the LORD went before them by day in a pillar of a cloud...' This angel of God's presence was no other than Jesus Christ, the conductor of them in the wilderness, who safe-guarded them, and secured them all the way from Egypt to Canaan.

And we Christians may also tempt Christ, for the apostle warneth us against it: we tempt Christ, now he is ascended into heaven, when we disobey his laws, question his authority, doubt of his promises, after sufficient means of conviction, that he is the Messiah, the Son of God; grow weary of his religion, loathing spiritual manna, and begin to be glutted with the gospel [to think that we have too much of it], and are discouraged in the way to our heavenly Canaan, whither we are travelling.

(3) The Holy Ghost is said also to be tempted: 'How is it that ye have agreed together to tempt the Spirit of the Lord?' (Acts 5:9) – namely, by their [Ananias and Sapphira] hypocrisy and dissimulation [pretence], putting it to the trial, whether he [the Spirit] could discover them in their sin, yea or no; they had endeavoured, as much as in them lay, to deceive the Spirit by keeping back part of the price; that is, by that practice they would put it to the trial, whether the Holy Ghost, yea or no, could find out that cheat and fallacy [deception]. It is not barely to deceive the apostles, who were full of the Holy Ghost, and had a discerning spirit, though to them they brought their lie. No, saith the apostle, 'Ye have not lied unto men, but unto God' (verse 4); and therefore they are said to 'tempt the Holy Ghost', whether he could find them out or no, though they had so many experiences of his care and respect to the church, and all affairs belonging thereunto; and so the injury was done, not to the apostles, but to the Holy Ghost himself.

2. *The act*

What is this temptation of God? Temptation is the proving and making trial of a thing or person, what he is, and what he will do. Thus we tempt God when we put it to the trial whether God will be as good as his word, and doubt of the comminatory [threatening] and promissory [promising] part thereof, or whether he will be such an one as he is taken to be. Now, this is lawful or unlawful according as the trial is made humble and dutifully, or else proudly and sinfully, whether God will do such a thing as we have prescribed him. And again, as the trial is made necessarily or unnecessarily. Sinfully we are said to tempt God when we make an unnecessary experiment of his truth, goodness and power, and care of us, having had sufficient assurance of these things before.

(1) There is a tempting or proving of God in a way of duty. So we are bidden: 'Bring ye all the tithes into the storehouse, that there may be meat in mine house, and prove me now therewith, saith the LORD of hosts, if I will not open you the windows of heaven, and pour you out a blessing, that there shall not be room enough to receive it' (Malachi 3:10). God there submitteth to a trial upon experience; though we are to believe him upon his bare word, yet he will have us to wait for the things promised; and in this sense it is said, 'The word of the LORD is a tried word, he is a buckler to all them that trust in him' (Psalm 18:30). All those that build any hope upon it, and wait to see what the Lord will do, will find that God will stand to [keep to] his word. This is a constant duty to observe God's truth and faithfulness. To suspend [If we suspend] our belief till the event [brings it to pass] is distrust; but to wait, observing what God will do as to the event, is an unquestionable duty.

(2) There is an allowed trying of God in some cases. I cannot say it is a duty, because it is only warrantable by God's special indulgence and dispensation; and I cannot say it is a sin, because of God's gracious condescension to his people: 'And Gideon said unto God, Let not thine anger be hot against me, and I will speak but this once: let me prove, I pray thee, but this once with the fleece; let it now be dry only upon the fleece, and upon all the ground let there be dew' (Judges 6:39). The request was not of distrust and malice, but of infirmity and from a weak faith; not out of infidelity to tempt God, but out of humility; being sensible of his own

weakness, he desired this help, for the further confirmation of his faith concerning his calling to this work, as an instrument authorised, and the issue and success of it; and also to assure others who followed him.

To this head I refer Thomas's proof and trial: 'Except I see in his hand the print of the nails, and put my finger into the print of the nails, and thrust my hand into his side, I will not believe' (John 20:25). Here was weakness in Thomas, to suspend his faith upon such a condition, but an apostle was to be *autoptes*, an eye-witness of those things which were done, especially of his resurrection; and therefore, Christ meekly condescended to his request: 'Reach hither thy finger, and behold my hands, and reach hither thy hand, and thrust it into my side, and be not faithless, but believing' (verse 27). I put it among infirmities: he alloweth him his trial of sense, and with some rebuke.

To this head [under this class] may be referred that [instance of] of Hezekiah, who, when he was sick of a mortal disease, and the Lord had extraordinarily promised him, on his mourning, that he should be recovered again, he asks a sign for the confirmation of his faith, and God grants it him (2 Kings 20:8, 9). And the instance of Ahaz, who, when the prophet bid him 'ask a sign', he said: 'I will not ask, neither will I tempt the LORD' (Isaiah 7:12). He believed nothing of what the prophet had spoke, and was resolved to go on in his way, but he pretended a reverent and religious respect to God. This kind of tempting God is tolerable, being an act of condescension in God to the weakness of his people.

(3) There is a sinful tempting of God, and this in done two ways:

(i) Generally every transgression, in a general sense, is a

tempting of God: 'They have tempted me now these ten times, and have not hearkened to my voice' (Numbers 14:22). Every eminent and notable provocation of theirs is called a tempting of God. Hereby they make trial of God's justice, whether he will execute vengeance upon them or no. Thus we tempt Christ when we fall into any voluntary and known sin, we put it to the trial what he will or can do; we enter into the lists with God, provoke him to the combat: 'Do we provoke the Lord to jealousy? are we stronger than he?' (1 Corinthians 10:22). We try whether God will be so severe as his threatening speaks him to be, as if we would make some experiment of his anger, justice and power. This kind of tempting of God is compounded of infidelity and presumption. There is infidelity in it when we dare sin against the clear light and checks [restraints] of conscience, and venture upon his threatenings. You cannot drive a dull ass into the fire that is kindled before him: 'Surely in vain the net is spread in the sight of any bird' (Proverbs 1:17). And there is presumption in it, therefore these voluntary acts of rebellion are called presumptuous sins: 'Keep back thy servant also from presumptuous sins' (Psalm 19:13). Gross and scandalous sinners are described to be such as tempt God: 'And now we call the proud happy; yea, they that work wickedness are set up; yea, they that tempt God are even delivered' (Malachi 3:15). And Ananias and Sapphira are said to 'tempt the Holy Ghost' (Acts 5:9). By open voluntary sins men dare God to his face; by secret sins we put it to the trial whether God be [is] an all-seeing God, and will discover this hypocrisy. Both [sorts of persons] conclude they shall do well enough, though they break his laws, and run wilfully upon evil practices forbidden by his law.

(ii) More particularly we tempt God [in] two ways: in a

way of distrust or presumption. Both these arise from unbelief, though they seem to be contrary extremes; for though presumption may seem to arise from an over-much confidence, yet if it be narrowly [carefully] searched into, we shall find that men presume upon unwarrantable courses [act sinfully], because they do not believe that God will do what is meet [fitting] to be done [by him] in his own time or in his own way. As, for instance, had the Israelites believed that God, in his own time, and in his own way, would have destroyed the Canaanites, they would not have presumed, against an express charge, to have gone against them without the ark and without Moses, as they did (Numbers 14:40-45); they presumed to go up unto the hill-top, and then they were discomfited [put to flight]. But presumption in some being most visible, in others distrust, therefore we make two kinds of them.

(a) *In a way of distrust.* And that is done several ways, but all agree in this: not content with what God hath done already to settle our faith, we prescribe means of our own, and indent with him [agree to serve] upon terms of our own making. So the Israelites, 'And he called the name of the place Massah and Meribah, because of the chiding of the children of Israel, and because they tempted the LORD, saying, Is the LORD among us, or not?' (Exodus 17:7). They had sufficient signs of God's presence: the pillar of a cloud and fire, that went before them by day and by night; but they would have signs of their own. So the Jews are said to tempt Christ, because they sought a sign from heaven: 'The Pharisees also, with the Sadducees, came, and, tempting, desired him that he would show them a sign from heaven' (Matthew 16:1). He had given sufficient evidence of his mission and divine power in casting out devils and healing the sick and diseased; but they would have a sign from heaven, some sign of their own prescribing. The devil is ready to put such thoughts into our minds. If God be with us, let him show it by doing this or that; and we are apt to require stronger proofs of God's power and presence with us than he alloweth. This is a frequent sin now-a-days, and men are many ways guilty of it.

First, Some will not believe the gospel except they see a miracle or hear an oracle. Christ representeth their thoughts: 'Nay, father Abraham, if one went to them from the dead, then they would repent' (Luke 16:30). They would have other ways of assurance than God alloweth, and are not content with his word and works, by which he revealeth himself to us, but will, at their own pleasure, make trial of his will and power, and then believe. These tempt God, and therefore no wonder if God will not do for them that which they require.

Secondly, Some will not believe God's providence, but make question of his power and goodness, and care over us and our welfare, when he hath given us sufficient proof thereof. When he hath taken care to convince our infidelity by supplying our wants, and hath done abundantly enough already for evidencing his power, justice, and truth, and readiness to help us, we will not believe unless he give us new and extraordinary proof of each, such as we prescribe to him: 'When your fathers tempted me, proved me, and saw my works. Forty years long was I grieved with this generation, and said, It is a people that do err in their hearts, and they have not known my ways' (Psalm 95:9, 10). They saw his works, were fed with miracles, and clothed with miracles, yet they must have new proof still. Two ways of tempting him as to his providence the scripture mentions:

One was their setting God a task of satisfying their conceits and carnal affections: 'And they tempted God in their hearts, by asking meat for their lusts' (Psalm 78:18). Of this sin they are guilty that must be maintained at such a rate, must have such provision for them and theirs, or else they cannot believe his truth and care of them. As the Israelites, God must give them festival diet in the wilderness, or else they will no longer believe his power and serve him.

The other way of tempting God, with respect to his providence, was by confining him to their own time, manner, and means of working: 'Yea, they turned back, and tempted God, and limited the Holy One of Israel' (Psalm 78:41). To limit the Holy One is to confine him within a circle of their own making, and if he doth not help them by their means, and at their time, as those in the text, they will not tarry God's leisure, they think there is no depending on him, for any succour [help]. Thus they set bounds to his wisdom and power, as if he could do no more than they conceive to be probable. Thus also we prescribe means and time to God, take upon us to set rules to him how he should govern the world. And one usual way of tempting God now is, when we will not go fair and softly in the path and pace of God's appointing, but are offended at the tediousness thereof, and make haste, and take more compendious ways of our own [short cuts]: 'He that believeth will not make haste' (Isaiah 28:16); but he that believeth not is precipitant [hasty], must have God's mercy, power, and goodness manifested to them in their own way and time.

Thirdly, Some will not be satisfied as to their spiritual estate [condition] without some sensible [tangible] proof, or such kind of assurance as God usually vouchsafeth [gives] not to his people. As suppose they must be fed with spiritual dainties, and overflow with sensible consolation in every holy duty, or else they are filled with disquieting thoughts about their acceptance with God. We must have matters of faith put under the view and feeling of sense, or else we will not take comfort in them. But we must not limit God to give proofs of his love, nor prescribe such signs as are not promised by him, but study our case in the Word. For God will not always treat us by sensible experience. Thomas is allowed to touch Christ, but Mary is not allowed to touch him (John 20:17, compared with verse 27).

(b) *In a way of presumption*; so we tempt God when, without any warrant, we presume of [on] God's power and providence. As here the devil tempted Christ to cast himself down from the pinnacle of the temple, to try if he would take charge of him in the fall; whereupon Christ replieth, 'Thou shalt not tempt the Lord thy God.' Now this is done several ways.

First, When we presume upon God's help, forsaking the ordinary way and means. Christ would not throw himself down, when he could go down by the stairs or steps of the temple. Downstairs and over the battlements is not all one [not one and the same thing]. Christ, that could walk upon the sea in the distress of his disciples, in ordinary cases taketh a ship. Whosoever will not use the ordinary means that God hath appointed, but in ordinary cases expects extraordinary supplies, tempteth God. God is able to bring water out of the rock, when there is nothing but rock and stone; but when we may hope to find spring-water, we must dig for it. God can rain manna out of heaven; but when the soil will bear corn, we must till it. When Elisha was in a little village, not able to defend him from the Syrians, he had chariots and horsemen of fire to defend him (2 Kings 6:17);

but when he was in Samaria, a strong, walled town, and the king of Israel sent to fetch his head [to behead him], he said to those that were with him, 'Shut the door' (verse 32). Christ in the wilderness miraculously fed many; but near the city he 'sent his disciples to buy bread' (John 4:8). When the Church of God had need of able helps at first, gifts[9] were miraculously conferred; but afterwards every man to his study: 'Meditate upon these things, give thyself wholly to them, that thy profiting may appear to all' (1 Timothy 4:15). In short, God's omnipotency is for that time discharged, when we have ordinary means to help ourselves. To disdain ordinary means, and expect extraordinary, is as if a man should put off his clothes, and then expect God should keep him from cold.

Secondly, When we expect the end without the means. If Hezekiah had refused the bunch of figs, or Paul's companions to tarry in the ship, they had [would have] tempted God. When we desire any blessing, we must not refuse or neglect any good means for attaining of it. In spiritual things this is very usual; men hope to have the end without the means. In temporal things we will soon confess there must be means used, for 'if any would not work, neither should he eat' (2 Thessalonians 3:10). In warfare no victory is to be hoped for without fighting; only in spiritual matters we think we do well enough, though we never put to our endeavours to cry [pray] for knowledge, and to dig [study the Bible and hear sermons] for it; this is a tempting of God: 'If thou criest after knowledge, and liftest up thy voice for understanding; if thou seekest her as silver, and searchest for her as for hid

---

9. Manton is referring to the Charismatic Gifts of the Early Church. He clearly expected these to be withdrawn.

treasures; then shalt thou understand the fear of the LORD, and find the knowledge of God' (Proverbs 2:3-5). We dream of [deceive ourselves that we shall get to] heaven when there is no mortification [stopping our sins], no exercising ourselves unto godliness. A great many say as Balaam did, 'Let me die the death of the righteous, and let my last end be like his' (Numbers 23:10); but they care not for living the life of the righteous. If they can but charm themselves into a secure presumption of salvation, they never give diligence to make their calling and election sure. This cometh from hardness of heart, not strength of faith. Many defer their conversion to the last, and then think that in the twinkling of an eye they shall in a trice [moment] be in heaven with Elias in whirlwind. It was a prayer of Sir Thomas More, *Domine, Deus, fac me in iis consequendis operam collocare, pro quibus obtinendis te orare soleo:* 'Lord! make me to bestow pains in getting those things, for the obtaining of which I use to pray [am in the habit of praying] to thee.' Otherwise we tempt God.

Thirdly, When without call we rush into any danger, or throw ourselves into it, with an expectation God will fetch us off [rescue] again. As if Christ, when nobody went about to thrust him down, should wilfully have cast himself down. Whether the danger be certain, or inevitable, or very probable, we must not throw ourselves on it; but, when God calls us, then we may expect his help according to his promise; as to go into places or houses infected [by disease]. In spiritual cases it is often done; men that by often [frequent] experience have found such and such things to be occasions to them of sinning, yet presume to do the same again; these tempt God, ride into the devil's quarters [territory], go into dangerous places and companies where they are like [likely] to be corrupted; as Peter went into the high-priest's hall, and those that go to live in Popish [Roman Catholic] families. We pray that we be not led into temptations, but when we lead ourselves, what shall become of us, as we do when we cast ourselves upon temptations, and dangerous occasions of sin?

Fourthly, When we undertake things for which we are not fitted and prepared, either habitually or actually: as to speak largely [preach for a considerable time] without meditation. When an unlearned man undertakes the handling a weighty controversy, and a good cause wanteth shoulders [an able person to defend it], we tempt God. When we undertake things above bodily strength, all will condemn us; so to undertake things that we have no ability to perform is unlawful. The sons of Sceva would take upon them to exorcise the devil, 'And the man in whom the evil spirit was leaped on them, and overcame them, and prevailed against them, so that they fled out of that house naked and wounded' (Acts 19:16).

Fifthly, Another sort of tempting God is, when we come to him with an idol in our hearts; that is, when people are resolved of a thing, they will go and ask counsel of God. In all matters we resolve on we are to take God's leave, and counsel, and blessing; but they first resolve and then ask God's counsel. And, therefore, God saith in Ezekiel 14:4: 'Every man of the house of Israel that setteth up his idols in his heart, and putteth the stumbling-block of his iniquity before his face, and cometh to the prophet, I the LORD will answer him that cometh according to the multitude of his idols.' Balaam had a mind to the wages of unrighteousness, but yet he durst not [did not dare] go without God, and, till God had permitted him, he would be asking again and again

(Numbers 22:12, compared with the 20th and 22nd verses). God answered him in wrath, according to the idol of his heart. Thus you see men tempt God, when, either out of diffidence or presumption, they seek an experience of his wisdom, power, justice, truth, goodness, against his word and command, and the order he hath established; as the Israelites, when means failed, murmured and prescribed time, means, and manner of deliverance, as if they would subject God to their lusts.

2. The heinousness of the sin

(1) Because it is a great arrogancy [form of pride] when we seek thus to subject the Lord to our direction, will and carnal affections. Prescribing to God argueth too great an ascribing [trusting] to ourselves. Certainly the Lord cannot endure that his people, who ought wholly to depend upon him, submit to him, and be ruled by him, should prescribe as they please how and when he should help them; and that his power and goodness should lacquey upon [be a slave to], and be at the beck [and call] of, our idle and wanton humours [sinful lusts]. The direction [government] of the affairs of the world is one of the flowers of God's crown.

Now to dislike of his holy government is a presumptuous arrogancy in the creature; we will take upon us to model our mercies and chose our means, and will not tarry the time that he hath appointed for our relief, but will anticipate it, and shorten it according to our fancies. God is sovereign, we are as clay in his hands; he is our potter, and must prescribe the shape in which we must be formed, and the use we must be put to: 'O house of Israel, cannot I do with you as the potter, saith the LORD? Behold as the clay is in the potter's hand, so are ye in mine hand, O house of Israel' (Jeremiah 18:6).

He hath full right to dispose of the creature as he pleaseth, and according to the counsel of his own will, to which we are to be subject without murmuring or repining [complaining]. We cannot say to him, 'What makest thou? or why dost thou this?' 'Woe unto him that striveth with his maker! let the potsherd strive with the potsherds of the earth: shall the clay say to him that fashioneth it, What makest thou? or thy work, He hath no hands' (Isaiah 45:9). Tempting before the event is the same almost with murmuring after the event.

(2) It is great unbelief, or a calling into question God's power, mercy and goodness to us. We should entirely depend upon God for salvation, and whatsoever is necessary to salvation, and that he will supply our wants, and bring us out of every strait [difficult experience], in a way most conducing to our own welfare and his honour. But now we are not satisfied with the assurance God hath given us in those laws of commerce [i.e. God's dealings], which are established between him and us. We must have extraordinary proofs, or else we question all. Tempting God seemeth rather to be opposed to the fear and reverence that we should have of him; yet primarily and in itself, it is rather opposite to our trust. And though we take it for a sin which argueth too much trust, or an unwarrantable boldness in expecting unusual ways of help from God, yet generally it belongeth to unbelief and diffidence, and ariseth from it. For, therefore, we put him to proof, tempt, or make trial of God, because we distrust his help, and are not satisfied with his goodness and power, till we have other testimonies thereof, than are ordinarily dispensed. Therefore this reason is given of their tempting God, because 'they believed not God, and trusted not in his salvation' (Psalm 78:22). They must have

their own salvation, their own way of supply or deliverance, or else they cannot trust God if he doth not help them at their time and by their means.

(3) It looseneth the bonds of all obedience, because we set up new laws of commerce [terms on which God must deal with us] between God and us; for when we suspect God's fidelity to us, unless he do such things as we fancy, we suspect our fidelity to him. Therefore disobedience is made the fruit of tempting God: 'Yea, they tempted and provoked the most high God, and kept not his testimonies' (Psalm 78:56). They that tempt God cast away God's rule, and God's terms and obedience, and make others to themselves. The question is, whether God shall direct us, or we him? We say, Unless God will do thus and thus, we will no longer believe his power and serve him.

(4) It is great ingratitude, or a lessening God's benefits and works already done for us: 'Behold he smote the rock, that the waters gushed out, and the streams overflowed; can he give bread also? can he provide flesh for his people?' (Psalm 78:20). As if what he had done formerly were nothing. Now, God cannot endure to have his benefits lessened, or his former works forgotten and despised.

(5) It is wantonness, rather than want, puts us upon tempting of God. There is a humour [common weakness] in men; we are very desirous to try conclusions, condemning things common, and are fond about strange novelties. It was told the Israelites, as plain as could be, that they should not reserve manna till the morning; and they need not to have reserved it, they had fresh every day; yet they would needs

keep it for experiment's sake, to try whether it would stink or no (Exodus 16:20). And though they were forbidden to gather it on the Sabbath day, having on the evening before enough for two days, and it was told them they should find none on the Sabbath day, yet they must try.

Where need is, there a man may commit himself to the providence of God, and rely upon him; and where means fail us, God can help us by prerogative, that we may say with Abraham, when we have no help present, 'In the mount of the LORD it shall be seen' (Genesis 22:14); and with Moses, when the Red Sea was before them, and the enemy was behind them, 'Fear ye not, stand still, and ye shall see the salvation of the LORD, which he will show to you today' (Exodus 14:13). When Elias was in distress, the angel brought him meat (1 Kings 19:5,6); when Hagar and Ishmael were in the wilderness, and the bottle spent, then God comforted her from heaven (Genesis 21:17); when the three children were in the fiery furnace, then God sent an angel to be their deliverer (Daniel 3:28).

But now, in wantonness to desire extraordinary proofs of God's care over us, when he hath in ordinary ways provided for us, is to tempt the Lord: 'They lusted exceedingly in the desert, and tempted God in the wilderness' (Psalm 106:14). When they had so many convictions of God's power and providence over them, which should in reason have charmed them into a full and cheerful resignation and dependence upon him, they, remembering the flesh-pots in Egypt, must have their luxuriant appetites gratified; and because they had not that festival plenty, which could not be expected in the wilderness, they reproached Moses for having brought them out of Egypt, to die in the wilderness; and now God must show them a miracle, not for the supply of their wants, but to pamper and feed their lusts: 'And they tempted God in their heart, by asking meat for their lust: yea, they spake against God; they said, Can God furnish a table in the wilderness?' (Psalm 78:18, 19). A table must be prepared; he must give them festival diet in the wilderness.

(6) It argues impatiency: 'They soon forgat his works; they waited not for his counsel, but lusted exceedingly in the wilderness, and tempted God in the desert' (Psalm 106:13, 14). The word signifies they made haste, took it ill they were not presently brought into that plenty that was promised: 'Wherefore have ye made us to come up out of Egypt, to bring us into this evil place? it is no place of seed, or of figs, or of vines, or of pomegranates, neither is there any water to drink' (Numbers 20:5), which was the plenty that was promised in the land of Canaan. Thus they made haste, were impatient of staying God's time of giving them this inheritance; and because they had it not presently, they wished themselves back again in Egypt. Tempting is because we cannot attend the performance of God's promise in his own time. They went out passionately in the pursuit of their plenty, which they looked for; and as soon as they discovered any difficulty, conclude they were betrayed, not waiting with patience God's time, when he should accomplish his promises made to them.

(7) The greatness of the sin is seen by the punishments of it. One is mentioned: 'Neither let us tempt Christ, as some of them also tempted, and were destroyed of serpents' (1 Corinthians 10:9). They were bitten of serpents, because they tempted God, and murmured because of the length of the way, that they could not get presently into Canaan; and

the apostle tells us that all the things which happened to Israel of old happened to them *hos typoi*, as patterns of providence. A people might easily read their own doom and destiny, if they would blow off the dust from the ancient providences of God, and observe what proofs and characters of his justice, wisdom, and truth are engraven there. The desert of sin is still the same, and the exactness of divine justice is still the same; and therefore what hath been is a pledge and document of what may be, if we fall into like crimes. God is impartially and immutably just; he is but one (Galatians 3:20). God is one, always consonant unto [consistent with] himself, and doth like unto himself [does what is fit]: his power is the same, so is his justice. Even the historical part of the Word is a kind of prophecy, not only a register and chronicle of what is past, but a kind of calendar and prognostication of what is to come. As other histories in scripture are left upon record for our learning, so especially the history of Israel's passage through the wilderness into Canaan.

Uses. Let us not tempt God in any of the kinds [ways] mentioned.

Use 1: Not by requiring new grounds of faith, when God hath given sufficient already; not by cherishing scepticism and irresolution in point of [the Christian] religion, till new nuncios [i.e. wonder-workers] come from heaven, with a power to work miracles, and to be endowed with extraordinary gifts, as the Seekers do.[10] Many waver in religion,

---

10. Seekers: name given to a seventeenth-century sect of Christians who taught that the Bible is not enough but that we also need to have miracles today to base our faith on.

would fain see an apparition, and have some extraordinary satisfaction, which God would not give them upon every trifling occasion. The Pharisees must have a sign from heaven; the Papists would have the Protestant teachers show their commission by miracles; the Jews would believe if Christ came down from the Cross. To suspend our faith till God gives us our own terms is to tempt God. In order to dispossess you of this conceit [foolish idea], consider:

(i) Signs and wonders done in one age and time for the confirmation of the true religion, should suffice all ages and times afterwards; and it is a tempting God to ask more signs and wonders for the confirmation of that truth, which is sufficiently confirmed already, if there be a good and safe tradition of these things to us. The giving of the law was attended with thunderings and lightnings, and the sound of a terrible trumpet (Exodus 19), by which means the law was authorised, and owned as proceeding from God.

Now, it was not needful this should be repeated in every age, as long as a certain report and records of it might convey it to their ears. In the setting up a new law, signs and wonders are necessary to declare it to be of God; but when the church is in the possession of it, these cease. So in the Christian church; when the gospel was first set on foot, it was then confirmed with signs and wonders, but now they are unnecessary. See the law and gospel compared:

> 'For if the word spoken by angels was stedfast, and every transgression and disobedience received a just recompense of reward; how shall we escape, if we neglect so great salvation; which at the first began to be spoken by the Lord, and was confirmed unto us by them that heard him; God also bearing them witness, both with signs and wonders, and with divers miracles, and gifts of the Holy Ghost, according to his own will?' (Hebrews 2:2-4).

(ii) If you had lived in the age of signs and wonders, there were hard hearts then, unbelievers then, and blasphemers then, and tempters of God then: 'Because they believed not in God, and trusted not in his salvation, though he had commanded the clouds from above, and opened the doors of heaven, and had rained manna upon them to eat, and had given them of the corn of heaven ... For all this they sinned still, and believed not for his wondrous works' (Psalm 78: 22-32). Extraordinary works will not work upon them upon whom ordinary works will not prevail.

Objection. But for them that have to do with the conversion of Indians and remote parts of the world, is it a tempting of God to ask the gift of miracles?

Answer. I cannot say so. God may be humbly sought unto about direction in the gifts of tongues and healing, being so necessary for the instruments employed, as well as the conviction of the nations. I dare not determine anything in the case, but I am satisfied with Acostus'[11] reasons why miracles are not afforded by God now, as well as in the primitive times. Then simple and unlearned men were sent to preach Christianity among the nations, where many were armed and instructed against it with all kind of learning and philosophy; but now learned men are sent to the ignorant, and are superior to them in reason, and in civility and authority; and, besides, present them a religion far more credible than their own, that they cannot easily withstand the light of it.

---

11. I find an Acosta who was an unorthodox seventeenth century Jew. But I find no Acostus. It seems to be a reference to an obscure writer.

Use 2: Do not run into any wilful and known sin, as if you would try how far the patience of God will go, nor abuse his fatherly goodness by going on still in your trespasses. When a man will try the patience of God without any regard of his threatenings, or the instances of his wrath, which are before his eyes, he puts it to the proof whether God will punish him, yea or no.

Remember you are no match for him: 'Woe unto him that striveth with his maker! let the potsherds strive with the potsherds of the earth' (Isaiah 45:9). As Abner said to Asahel in 2 Samuel 2:21, 22: 'Turn thee aside to thy right hand or to thy left, and lay thee hold on one of the young men, and take thee his armour. But Asahel would not turn aside from following him. And Abner said again to Asahel, Turn thee aside from following me: wherefore should I smite thee to the ground?'

So if you will needs be tempting and trying conclusions, and making experiments, let men meddle with their match, those who are equal to themselves, not challenging one infinitely above them. Let frail man cope with man, but let him take heed of meddling with God: 'Can thine heart endure, or can thine hands be strong in the days that I shall deal with thee?' (Ezekiel 22:14).

Many foolish people say, as those in the prophet, 'It is an evil, and I must bear it'; endure it as well as I can. What! endure the loss of heaven! endure the wrath of the Almighty God! If Rachel could not endure the loss of her children, nor Jacob the supposed loss of Joseph, but, says he, 'I will go down into the grave unto my son mourning' (Genesis 37:35); if Achitophel could not endure the rejectment of his counsel, and Haman could not endure to be slighted by Mordecai, and many cannot endure the loss of a beloved child; how wilt thou endure the loss of eternal happiness? The disciples wept bitterly when Paul said, 'Ye shall see my face no more' (Acts 20:38). What will ye do, then, when God shall say, Ye shall see my face no more?

Ah wretch! how canst thou endure the wrath of God? Thou canst not endure to be scorched a few days with feverish flames; thou canst not endure the acute pains of [the gall] stone and gout, when God armeth the humours of thine own body against thee [takes away health]; thou canst not endure the scorching of a little gunpowder casually blown up; thou canst not endure the pains of a broken arm or leg; and can you endure the wrath of God, when God himself shall fall upon you with all his might?

Use 3: When we are destitute and sorely distressed, let us wait upon God with patience, according to the tenor of his promises, and tarry his leisure, without prescribing time and means. God knoweth the fittest season, and delighteth oftentimes to show our impatience and try our faith: 'O woman, great is thy faith!' (Matthew 15:28). And that his help may not be ascribed to chance or our industry, and that we may the more prize blessings, consider you cannot be more distressed than Christ was, who seemed abandoned to Satan's power, distressed with sore hunger through his long fasting. The devil was permitted to have power over his body, to carry him to one of the pinnacles of the temple, and yet he discovered an invincible confidence and trust in God, that he would not step the least step out of God's way for his preservation in so imminent a danger.

Now that you may not tempt God:
(1) Let your heart be deeply possessed with apprehensions of the goodness, wisdom and power of God. The scripture

telleth us for his goodness: 'Thou art good, and doest good' (Psalm 119:68); and again: 'The LORD is good to all' (Psalm 145:9). For his wisdom: 'He is wonderful in counsel, and excellent in working' (Isaiah 28:29). His purposes are often hidden from us, but he doeth all things well; God can do more for us than seemeth probable at the present; and therefore let us not tempt him by confining him to our time, means and manner. He may love us, and yet delay our help: 'Jesus loved Lazarus', and yet, 'When he heard that he was sick, he abode two days still in the same place where he was' (John 11:5, 6). Then, for his power and sovereign dominion, there is not a better argument for confidence than the preface and conclusion of the Lord's Prayer. Whatsoever state you are reduced to, God is still to be trusted, who is 'Our Father, which is in heaven', and 'whose is the kingdom, power, and glory'. 'I know whom I have believed, and I am persuaded that he is able to keep that which I have committed unto him against that day' (2 Timothy 1:12). Whatsoever our straits [difficulties] be, he is a God still to be trusted.

(2) Be firmly persuaded of God's care and providence over his people, and so careth for you in particular. This is assured to us by promises and by experiences. By promises: 'Casting all your care upon him, for he careth for you' (1 Peter 5:7); 'Be careful for nothing: but in everything by prayer and supplication, with thanksgiving, let your requests be made known unto God; and the peace of God, which passeth all understanding, shall keep your hearts and minds through Jesus Christ' (Philippians 4:6, 7). By experiences: 'O ye of little faith! why reason ye among yourselves, because ye have brought no bread? Do ye not yet understand, neither remember the five loaves of the five thousand,

and how many baskets ye took up?' (Matthew 16:8, 9). Christ was angry with his disciples, that they should be troubled about bread, since they had lately such experience of his power to provide bread at pleasure. Use the means God puts into your hands, and refer the success to him. You need not be anxious about anything in this world.

(3) Let all this produce in you an holy obstinacy of trust and obedience, or an invincible confidence in God, and close adherence to him, whatever your dangers, straits, and extremities be, and this will guard your heart against all tempting of God:

(i) A resolute trust and dependence: 'Though he slay me, yet will I trust in him' (Job 13:15). This is the soul that is prepared to be true to God, and contentedly to bear whatever he sendeth.

(ii) A constant adherence to our duty: 'Wait on the LORD, and keep his way' (Psalm 37:34). Do not go one step out of God's way for all the good in the world. The greatest extremities are to be borne rather than the least sin yielded to: 'Our God, whom we serve, is able to deliver us from the burning fiery furnace; and he will deliver us out of thine hand, O king. But if not, be it known unto thee, O king, that we will not serve thy gods, nor worship the golden image which thou hast set up' (Daniel 3:17, 18). Please God, and God will be always with you, when you seem to be left destitute: 'And he that sent me is with me: the Father hath not left me alone; for I do always those things that please him' (John 8:29).

5

Again, the devil taketh him up into an exceeding high mountain, and showeth him all the kingdoms of the world, and the glory of them; and saith unto him, All things will I give thee, if thou wilt fall down and worship me (Matthew 4:8, 9).

This is the third temptation. In handling it I shall use the former method, give you the history of the temptation, and observations thereupon. In the history: (1) The introduction (verse 8); (2) The temptation itself, with the grievousness of it (verse 9); (3) Christ's reply (verse 10).

1. In the introduction we have: (1) The place the devil taketh him unto: *an exceeding high mountain*; (2) The fact: *he showeth him all the kingdoms of the world, and the glory of them.*

(1) The place chosen for the conflict, 'an exceeding high mountain'. For the mountain, the scripture would not name it, and we need not anxiously inquire after it, whether any near Jericho, as some say, or as others, some mountain near Jerusalem; and possibly the highest above the rest was chosen by the tempter. The pinnacle of the temple was not proper [suitable], because Jerusalem was surrounded with higher mountains on all sides: 'As the mountains are round about Jerusalem' (Psalm 125:2). He chose an high mountain, because of the fairer prospect, where the horizon might be as spacious as was possible, and the sight not hindered by

any interposing object. God took Moses into Mount Pisgah, and showed him the land of Canaan (Deuteronomy 34:1). The devil, who affecteth to do in evil as God doth in what is good, taketh Christ into a mountain. He leadeth us high, and promiseth us high things, that suiteth with his disposition; but it endeth in a downfall that suiteth with his condition. The close is still 'cast thyself down', or else, as here, 'fall down and worship me'. The devil's taking him up thither is to be explained the same way with his taking him up to the pinnacle of the temple.

(2) The fact, and 'showeth him all the kingdoms of the world, and the glory of them'. But how could the devil from one mountain show him all the kingdoms of the world, when there is none so high as that we can see the latitude of one kingdom, much less through all, partly through the unequal swellings of the earth, and partly through the weakness of the eye, which cannot reach so far? The sight could go no further than the horizon, and the other hemisphere is not to be seen at all; that part which we see is much less than that part which we see not. Therefore how could he show him all the kingdoms of the world, and the glory thereof? *Answer*. These words must not be taken rigorously; but that he showed them: (i) *In compendio* [in brief compass]; (ii) *In speculo* [in a vision]; (iii) *In colloquio* [in conversation].

(i) *In compendo* [in brief compass]. It may be understood of so many kingdoms as could fall under the sight of a man looking round about him from some eminent place; as God is said to show Moses all the land of Canaan, when he did actually see only a part thereof. From that high mountain the devil gave him a view of all that was to be seen from thence; many castles, towns, and fruitful fields might be seen as a sample of the rest. It is a synechdochical hyperbole [an exaggerated expression, a part being taken for the whole], he that showeth a part of a thing, and the chiefest part, may be said to show the thing itself.

(ii) *In speculo* [in a vision], besides what he might reach by his sight. By way of representation and external visible species, he represented to Christ all the rest of the kingdoms of the world and the pomp and glory thereof as in a map. For Satan can object [present] to the eyes of men the species [vision] and images of divers [all sorts of] things; and there is no absurdity to think that in this way he showed his utmost art and cunning to represent the world to Christ in as splendid and inviting a manner as he could. If you ask, therefore, why he carried him to a high mountain – he might have done this in a valley or any other place as well? I answer, it is true that if the discovery [revelation] had been only by representation, or if the devil could have deluded Christ's fancy or imagination, so as to impress these species [visions] upon it so far as that he should seem to see what he did not see, [then] a valley would have served turn as well as a mountain. But this was done without it, and [yet as if] with it, showing the glory of the world as in a map and picture, and therefore a convenient place is chosen.

(iii) *In colloquio,* by discourse. The temptation might be helped on by the devil's pointing at the several quarters of the world, with words relating the glory thereof, what splendour and glory the kings and nations had which adored him, all which Christ should have if he would fall down and worship him. Now all this while Satan is but making way for his purpose, thinking Christ would be ravished with this glorious sight. Possibly it was not a mere dumb show, but the tempting objects were amply set forth by Satan's speech.

2. The temptation itself, where we may consider the nature and the grievousness of it.

1. *The nature of the temptation*, where observe two things:
(1) An offer or a promise: *all these things will I give thee*;
(2) A postulation or demand: *if thou wilt fall down and worship me.*

(1) An offer or promise: 'all these things will I give thee.' This is a vain boast of the tempter, who ascribeth to himself that which was proper to God, and promiseth to Christ those things which were all his before. God had said in Psalm 2:8: 'Ask of me, and I will give thee the heathen for thine inheritance, and the uttermost parts of the earth for thy possession.' This the devil, who affecteth to be like God, arrogateth unto himself, as if he would make him the universal king of the world. In Luke 4:6 it is: 'All this power will I give thee, and the glory of them; for that is delivered unto me, and to whomsoever I will I give it.' But you must not always look for truth in the devil's speeches; he is not lord of the world to dispose of it as his own pleasure. And yet it is not to be supposed he would come with a downright untruth to the Son of God, if there were no pretence or varnish for it. Therefore we must distinguish between the devil's lie and the colour thereof.

(i) Certain it is that God doth govern all the affairs of this world, and doth put bounds and limits to Satan's power, beyond which he cannot pass, and doth often hinder his endeavours, and turn them to the quite contrary end and purpose; and if he doth not hinder them, yet he directeth them for good to his people. Therefore that power that Satan hath is not given, but permitted; not absolute, but limited. It is a lie that Satan can give these things at pleasure; see these scriptures: 'The earth is the LORD's, and the fulness thereof; the world, and they that dwell therein' (Psalm 24:1); 'He changeth the times and the seasons; he removeth kings, and setteth up kings' (Daniel 2:21); and verse 37, 'The God of heaven hath given thee a kingdom, power, and strength, and glory.' All the alterations that are in the earth are of the Lord; he pulleth down, and raiseth up, as seemeth good unto him. Therefore this power of disposing kingdoms belongeth unto God.

(ii) That the Son of God is the right heir of the world: 'Whom he hath appointed heir of all things' (Hebrews 1:2). To whom the nations are given: 'Ask of me, and I will give thee the heathen for thine inheritance, and the uttermost parts of the earth for thy possession' (Psalm 2:8); 'All power is given unto me in heaven and in earth' (Matthew 28:18). And therefore it was impudence in him to arrogate this power, and to promise these things to the Lord which were his before.

(iii) Though this was a lie, yet here is the colour of the lie. God permitteth that men sometimes by indirect means become great in honour and dignity in this world; all which are done by the instinct [impulse (?)] of Satan and his help. And evil men often succeed in their attempts, and from hence Satan is called the prince of this world: 'The prince of this world cometh, and hath nothing in me' (John 14:30); 'Of judgment, because the prince of this world is judged' (John 16:11). Yea, Paul goeth higher, and calleth him 'the god of this world': 'In whom the god of this world hath blinded the minds of them which believe not' (2 Corinthians 4:4). But this is by usurpation, not just right. And the devils are called, 'The rulers of the darkness of this world' (Ephesians 6:12), as the wicked consent to his empire and evil suggestions. But all this implieth but a limited and restrained kingdom; and the devil's impudence and falsehood lieth in this, that he interprets God's permission for a commission, his connivance for a conveyance [entitlement]. Indeed, there are two lies in the devil's offer: one assertory, as if the power and glory of the world were at his disposal; the other promissory, as if he would invest Christ in the full and peaceable possession thereof; whereas indeed he went about to divest and dispossess the Son of God of his right, or to tempt him to do a thing contrary to his kingdom. For he knew the abasement of Christ was the way to his glory, the cause of man's happiness, and the ruin of the kingdom of the devil; therefore he seeketh to prevent this by these magnificent promises.

(2) The postulation or demand: 'if thou wilt fall down and worship me'. Here the devil appeareth in his own likeness. Before it was, 'if thou be the Son of God'; now it is, 'fall down and worship me'. Before he appeared as a friend to advise him in his hunger; then as a divine [preacher] to instruct him how to discover himself as the Messiah; now as a plain usurper of God's worship. And he demands but one act of prostration, such as was given to the kings of the East; and the Jews in that manner did worship God. Therefore this was the vilest and most blasphemous suggestion which Satan could devise, that the Son of God should stoop to God's rebel. Here we see the devil not only importunate, but impudent.

2. *The grievousness of the temptation*, that will appear in these considerations:

(1) Because it was represented in a matter grateful and pleasing. It was unnecessary to turn stones into bread, dangerous to throw himself down from a pinnacle of the temple; but it might seem sweet and grateful [welcome] to behold the kingdoms of the world and the glory thereof; for surely the glory of the world is a bewitching object, and would much move a carnal heart [i.e. the heart of a non-Christian]. And therefore he produceth this tempting object, and sets it before Christ himself. Mark [Notice], he showed him the glory only, not the burdens, the labours, the cares, those storms of jealousy and envy which those encounter with who are at the top. This way did he now choose wherewith to assault Christ. Had he really represented the world, with all the vexations attending it, the temptation had not been so great; but he showeth the kingdoms of the world, and the glory thereof: the bait, not the hook; he talketh highly of small things, commendeth what is pleasing, but hideth the bitter of these luscious sweets. He offereth Christ the glory of the kingdoms of the world, but dissembleth [conceals] the cares, the troubles, the dangers. Alas! we see the best side of those that live in courts, their gorgeous apparel, their costly entertainments, their power and greatness; but their fears of being depressed [put down] by superiors, jostled by equals, undermined by inferiors, are hidden from us.

Therefore the temptation was dexterously [skilfully] managed by the devil, in that he showed him the kingdoms of the world and the glory thereof. Temptations of the right hand are more dangerous than those of the left hand.

(2) He showeth the bait before he offereth the temptation, that the world might speak for him before he spake for himself, and prepared the mind of Christ by this bewitching object before he cometh either with his offer or demand. And then afterwards, before he maketh his demand, he premiseth [introduces] his offer: 'All these things will I give thee'. The offer is made before the spiteful [sinful] condition is mentioned. Observe the different methods of Christ and Satan: Satan maketh show of glory first, but Christ of the cross. Satan offereth the benefit before he seemeth to require the service, as here he doth first offer and then ask; but fallaciously, for indeed he requireth a present act, but only promiseth a future compensation: 'I will give thee' all these things. Christ telleth us the worst at first: 'If any man will come after me, let him deny himself, and take up his cross, and follow me' (Matthew 16:24). The issue showeth the fraud of the tempter, and the misery of those poor deluded souls who hearken [listen] to him. On the contrary, the sincerity of our Lord, and the happiness of those who obey him, will soon appear. The devil will have all paid before he parts with anything; no worship, no glory. But I am carried too far: my purpose was only to show his dexterity and cunning, how he sets a colour upon sin before he mentions it, by glorious promises, and the manifold pleasure and profit which comes by it.

(3) He doth not seek to move him by naked words, but by the sight of the thing itself. Objects move the senses, senses draw away the mind; nor are they the porters of the soul so much as the corrupters: 'Turn away mine eyes from beholding vanity, and quicken thou me in thy way' (Psalm 119:37). If we let loose our senses without a guard, we soon contract

a deadness of heart. There is nothing so soon led away as the eye, it is the broker [intermediary] between the heart and the object; the eye gazeth and the heart lusteth; this is the window by which Satan hath crept in, and all manner of taint hath been conveyed into the soul.

In the first sin, Eve was corrupted this way: 'And when the woman saw that the tree was good for food, and that it was pleasing to the eyes ... she took of the fruit thereof, and did eat' (Genesis 3:6). Gazing on the fruit with delight, her heart was ensnared. We read of Potiphar's wife: 'She cast her eyes on Joseph' (Genesis 39:7); of Achan: 'When I saw among the spoils a goodly Babylonish garment, and two hundred shekels of silver, and a wedge of gold of fifty shekels weight, then I coveted them, and took them' (Joshua 7:21). First he *saw*, then he *coveted*, then he *took* them, then he *hid* them, then Israel falls, and he is attached by lot. So it is said of Shechem and Dinah: 'He saw her, and took her, and lay with her, and defiled her' (Genesis 34:2). So of Samson: 'He went to Gaza, and saw there an harlot, and went in unto her' (Judges 16:1). David was ensnared by his eyes: 'From the roof he saw a woman washing herself, and the woman was very beautiful to look upon' (2 Samuel 11:2). Naboth's vineyard was ever in Ahab's eye, as being near his palace; therefore he is troubled and falls sick for it (1 Kings 21:1,2).

Now, because so many have been betrayed by their senses, the devil taketh this way to tempt Christ, as knowing this is the next way to the heart.

(4) He taketh him into an high mountain, that he might look far and near, and see the more provinces, cities and kingdoms, to move him the more. The devil was sensible [well

aware] that small things were not to be offered to Christ, and therefore dresseth out the temptation in as glorious a manner as he can.

The chapman of souls [Satan] is grown thirsty of late. He doth not offer all the kingdoms of the earth and the glory thereof. He knoweth that we will accept of less with thanks. The devil buyeth many at a very easy price; he needeth not carry them so high as the mountain; they are contented with a little gain that is got by a fraudulent bargain in the shop. If we stand in our window, or at our doors, we meet with temptations enough to carry us away. He needeth not come with kingdoms, or with the glory of all the world: thirty pence, the price of a slave, is enough to make Judas betray his master (Matthew 26:15); and the prophet telleth us of some that will transgress for handfuls of barley and pieces of bread (Ezekiel 13:19). And those pretended prophets, too, making God the author and maintainer of their lies and deceits. And, again, of those that respect persons, whether magistrates or ministers: 'To have respect of persons is not good: for, for a piece of bread will that man transgress' (Proverbs 28:21). And another prophet telleth us of those that 'sell the poor for a pair of shoes' (Amos 2:6 and 8:6). Those will take any price. And the apostle saith of Esau: 'For one morsel of meat he sold his birthright' (Hebrews 12:16). So that the devil may abate [take down] a great deal of what he offered Christ. He need not say to such, You shall have 'all these things'. Nay, hold you! You shall have this petty gain, that slight pleasure and carnal satisfaction.

It is a wonder to consider what small things make up a temptation to many, yea, to most. The world is so corrupt that they will violate conscience with a small hire. We are not tempted with great things. less will serve the turn. But the devil knew that small matters were no temptation to Christ, therefore he carrieth him to the mountain, that he might see the glory of all the earth, to make the temptation the more strong.

(5) He showeth him the kingdoms of the world (*en stigmei chronou*, Luke 4:5), in a moment of time – that circumstance is not to be passed over. When many objects and glorious come together of a sudden, they do the more surprise us. Therefore, the more to affect Christ with the splendour of these things, and on a sudden to prevail upon him, which otherwise he [the devil] was not likely to do, he did not represent the glory of these kingdoms of the world to Christ that he [Christ] might set them one after another, but all together, that there might be less time for consideration, that so his mind might be the more blinded by the appearing splendour of the tempting object, and his heart the more captivated thereby. Diverse things seen in one view do more surprise us than if viewed by a leisurely contemplation. Alas! we are sometimes overborne by the violence of a temptation, sometimes overtaken by the suddenness of it: Galatians 6:1, 'Brethren, if one be overtaken in a fault' *[prolemphthei]*, inconsiderately and suddenly surprised by a sin. We do many things preposterously and in haste, which we repent of by [at] leisure. Thus the devil thought to surprise Christ, but he [Christ] was aware of him.

(6) In other temptations the tempter doth only ask a thing to be done, but here he doth ask and promise things glorious, profitable, and pleasing to carnal sense, and such as seem every way desirable. The offers of gain and glory are promised to the temptation.

(7) He craveth but one thing, a very small thing, and this under the hope of the greatest advantage: one act of external adoration, easy to be performed; if Christ would but kneel to him, not as supreme God; an inferior adoration would have contented him: yield but a little, do but 'fall down and worship', it shall be enough. As the heathens of old said to the Christians, Do but touch the censer.[12] The commendation of God's servants was, that 'they had not bowed the knee to Baal' (Romans 11:4). The devil knoweth if he can get us to a little he shall get us to more; and the least reverence is too much to such an impure spirit.

Observations
(1) Observe from that [phrase] 'again the devil taketh him', that we must expect not only to be tempted, but to be often tempted. Satan hath both his wiles and darts (Ephesians 6:11, 16). He sometimes assaulteth us with the one, sometimes with the other. Therefore:

(i) Be not secure, but watch, and stand upon your defence. It is a careless soul that can sleep in so great a danger. There is yet a malicious tempting devil alive, who would 'sift you as wheat' (Luke 22:31); and somewhat within you which would betray you to him if you be not wary; and you may meet with such snares as you have not yet met withal [with].

(ii) Be not overmuch troubled and dejected if you be assaulted afresh. You must make your way to heaven almost every step by conflict and conquest. Remember your baptismal vow, the obligation of which ceaseth not till your life be ended; and then you shall be out of gunshot and harm's way

---

12. The Christians of Roman times were in this way tempted by the authorities to save themselves from persecution by committing a 'small' sin.

[temptation and trouble]. Therefore still follow the Captain of your salvation wherever he leadeth you. The more trials, the more glory.

(iii) Avoid rash judgment and censure, if the same happen to others. Pirates do not use to set upon an empty vessel. The best are most assaulted. God permitteth it for their trial, and Satan hath the greatest spite at them.

(2) Observe, That the more grievous temptations follow the lighter ones, and the last assaults and trials are usually the greatest. This is so, if you respect either the dexterity and cunning of the tempter, represented before, or the foulness of the temptation, that is, to idolatry. The best of God's children may be tempted to the most execrable [loathsome] sins. Thus usually doth Satan reserve his worst assaults for the last, and his last temptation is commonly the sorest. Dying beasts bite shrewdly; so Satan rageth most when he hath but a short time. Therefore, since our warfare is not over, let us prepare for the worst brunt [attack], and the last efforts of Satan. If God will crown us fighting, we have no cause to complain. Many of God's servants, whom he [Satan] could not draw to worldliness, sensuality, or vainglory in their lifetime, he will seek to inject blasphemous thoughts into their minds at last. But, though it be grievous, be not dismayed, your conquest is sure and near.

(3) Observe, The world and worldly things are the bait and snare which the tempter offereth to Christ and his followers. As here, when he would make his last onset upon Christ, he sets before him 'the kingdoms of the world, and the glory of them', as the matter of the temptation.

(i) There are three enemies of our salvation, the devil, the world and the flesh: they are reckoned up together: 'Wherein in time past ye walked according to the course of this world, according to the prince of the power of the air, the spirit that now worketh in the children of disobedience. Among whom also we all had our conversation in times past in the lusts of our flesh, fulfilling the desires of the flesh and of the mind' (Ephesians 2:2, 3). The devil is the deceiver and grand architect of all wickedness; the flesh is the principle that he worketh upon, or that rebelling faculty within us that would be pleased before God [i.e. in preference to doing God's will]; the world is the bait by which the devil would deceive us and steal away our hearts from God, for it suiteth with our fleshy appetites and desires.

More distinctly that Satan is an enemy appeareth from his name, that signifieth an adversary, and in many places of scripture he is so called; as Matthew 22:18: 'While men slept, the enemy came and sowed tares among the wheat', compared with the 39th verse, 'the enemy that sowed them is the devil'. He is the great enemy to God and man: 'Your adversary the devil like a roaring lion walketh about ...' (1 Peter 5:8).

The flesh is an enemy, yea, our greatest enemy, for it warreth against the soul: 'Abstain from fleshly lusts, which war against the soul' (1 Peter 2:11). Yea, it warreth against the spirit or better part, as contrary to it: 'For the flesh lusteth against the spirit, and the spirit against the flesh' (Galatians 5:17): other things could do us no harm without our own flesh. We are tempted to sin by Satan, encouraged to sin by the example and custom of the world, but inclined to sin by our own flesh.

The world is an enemy of our salvation, as well as the devil and the flesh; all the other enemies get strength by it.

By the bait of worldly things the devil pleaseth the flesh; we are in continual danger of being everlastingly undone by it. Whosoever is a lover of the world is presumed to be a professed enemy of God: 'Know ye not that the friendship of the world is enmity with God? Whosoever will be a friend of the world is the enemy of God' (James 4:4); 'If any man love the world, the love of the Father is not in him' (1 John 2:15). It is an enemy, because it keepeth us from God, who is our chief good, and the enjoyment of him among his blessed ones, which is our last end. There is a neglect of God and heavenly things where the world prevaileth.

(ii) The devil maketh use of the world to a double end.

[1] To divert us from God and heavenly things, that our time, and care, and thoughts may be wholly taken up about things here below: 'Soul, thou hast much goods laid up for many years; take thine ease, eat, drink and be merry' (Luke 12:19); 'They mind earthly things; but our conversation is in heaven' (Philippians 3:19, 20). These are perfectly opposite. Some are of the world, and speak of the world, and wholly mind the world, and are governed by the spirit of this world. They seldom look higher, or [if they do, only] very coldly and slightly. Thus that which should be thought of in the first place is scarce thought of at all. But, remember, he [Satan] doth but offer you worldly things to deprive you of heavenly.

[2] To draw us to some open sin for the world's sake, as here he tempted Christ to idolatry, and Demas to defection from the faith: 'Demas hath forsaken us, having loved this present world' (2 Timothy 4:10). Others to some carnal, fraudulent, oppressive course, whereby they are spotted by the world. The whore of Babylon propoundeth her abominations 'in a golden cup' (Revelation 17:4); and the great

motive here is, 'All this will I give thee'. Though the devil cometh not in person to us with his offers, he doth by his instruments; as Balak, when he sent to Balaam to curse the Israelites, he promised him great rewards: 'I will promote thee unto very great honour, and I will do whatsoever thou sayest unto me: come therefore, I pray thee, curse me this people' (Numbers 22:17). So when he doth entice you by the motions of your own hearts to anything that is unlawful, to falsehood, deceit, or unjust gain, or to get and keep wealth by any base or unjust means, or doing something that is base and unworthy of your religion.

[3] I observe that temptations from the world may prevail with us. Satan maketh use of a twofold artifice. The one is to greaten [enlarge] the worldly object, the other is to make us large promises of success, happiness, and contentment in our evil enterprises.

(a) He useth this sleight here; he doth in the most enticing manner lay the world before Christ as a splendid object, to greaten it in Christ's thoughts and apprehensions. Therefore, when we begin to magnify the riches, pomp and pleasures of the world, the devil is at our elbow, and we are running into the snare. And therefore, if we begin to say, 'Happy is the people that is in such a case', it is time to correct ourselves and say, 'Yea, happy is the people whose God is the LORD' (Psalm 144:15). Take heed the devil doth not gain this advantage over you, to make you follow the world with the greatest earnestness, and spiritual and heavenly things in a slight and overly manner. Esteem, desires, resolutions of worldly greatness, though not upon base conditions, begin the temptation. You think it is a fine thing to live in pomp and at ease, to swim in pleasures, and begin to resolve to make it your business. The devil hath you upon the hip [i.e. has got the advantage]; it is an hour of temptation.

(b) His next course is to make large offers and promises by his instruments or your own thoughts, that though you neglect God and heaven, and do engage in some sinful course, you shall do well in the world, and enjoy full satisfaction. There is a double evil in Satan's offers and promises:

First, they are false and fallacious: 'All these things will I give thee'. Satan maketh fair offers of what he cannot perform. He promiseth many things, but doth only promise them. He offereth the kingdoms of the world to Christ, but cannot make good his word; he showeth them to Christ, but cannot give them. And this is the devil's wont [usual practice], to be liberal in promises, to fill the minds of those that hearken to him with vain hopes, as if he could transfer the riches and honours of the world to whom he pleaseth, whereas they are shamefully disappointed, and find their ruin in the very things in which they sought their exaltation, and their projects are crossed, for 'the earth is the LORD's, and the fulness thereof' (Psalm 24:1).

Secondly, all the devil's offers and promises have a spiteful [sinful] condition annexed. He pretendeth to give, but yet selleth at the dearest rates. It is but a barter and exchange; a flat bargain, but no gift. He must have our souls, God is dishonoured, his laws broken, his Spirit grieved. The devil staineth his grant with unjust covenants, and exacteth more than the thing is worth.

Two ways then must we defeat the temptation:

(1) Not believing his promises, that I must be beholden to [obliged to] sin to make me happy. Those that by unlawful means get up to honour and wealth seem to have accepted

the devil's offer; they think he is lord of the world, and all the kingdoms and the glory thereof. Do not look upon wealth as the devil's gift, as a thing to be gotten by fraud, flattery, corruption, bribery: alas! it is put into 'bags with holes' (Haggai 1:6). It is called the 'deceitfulness of riches' (Matthew 13:22). They promise that contentment and happiness which they cannot give. There is sure dependence on the Lord's, but none on Satan's promises. Young men that are to begin the world, take up this resolution: take what God sendeth, but resolve never to take wealth out of Satan's hands; what God sendeth in the fair way of his providence, by his blessing on your lawful endeavours: 'The hand of the diligent maketh rich' (Proverbs 10:4); and verse 22, 'The blessing of the LORD it maketh rich, and he addeth no sorrow with it.' When you deal righteously, and do not barely heap up treasure to yourselves, but seek to grow rich toward God, to subordinate all to heaven and a better pursuit: otherwise God can find a moth and a thief for your estates [riches].

(2) The other way is, to consider what a sad bargain you make by gratifying the devil, and hearkening to his counsel: 'What is a man profited, if he shall gain the whole world, and lose his own soul? Or what shall a man give in exchange for his soul?' (Matthew 16:26). A man never gets anything with Satan, but he shall lose that which is more precious; he never maketh a proffer to our advantage, but to our loss and hurt. Follow the world as hard as you can, lie, cozen [beguile], cheat, and you shall be rich; put the case, It is so, but I must lose my soul, not in a natural, but legal sense: 'What is the hope of the hypocrite, though he hath gained, when God taketh away his soul?' (Job 27:8). He hath far better things from us than we have from him; a birthright for a mess of pottage, the hopes of heaven for an opulent [wealthy]

condition here below. The bird buys the fowler's [bird-catcher's] bait at a dear rate when his life must go for it. Thy soul must be lost, which all the gold and silver in the world cannot redeem and recover.

(4) I observe again that Christ by his refusal hath taught us to tread the world under our feet, and all the glory of it should be an ineffectual and cold motive to a sanctified soul. If we have the same spirit that was in Christ, it will be so. All the kingdoms of the world, and the glory of them, was far too little to make up a temptation to him. A mortified heart [one that masters sin] will contemn all this in comparison of our duty to God, and the comfort of a good conscience, and the hopes of glory. Surely they have not the spirit of Christ who are taken with small things, with a Babylonish garment, or some petty temptation.

Uses. The use [practical application] is to teach us how to counterwork [resist] Satan.

Use 1: Since he worketh upon the fleshy mind, we are to be mortified and grow dead to the world. We profess faith in a crucified Lord; we must be like him, crucified as he was crucified; then shall we glory in the cross of Christ, when we feel the virtue of it, and are planted into the likeness of it: 'God forbid that I should glory, save in the cross of our Lord Jesus Christ, by whom the world is crucified unto me, and I unto the world' (Galatians 6:14). Grow more dead to the riches, honour, pomp, pleasure, the favour, fear, love, wrath, praise and dispraise [disapproval and criticism] of men, that we may readily deny these things, so far as opposite to the kingdom of Christ, or our duty to God, or as they lessen our affections to him. We die as our esteem of those things doth decay; till the man's temper be altered there is no hope to prevail by argument. Only they that are made partakers of a divine nature do escape the corruption that is in the world through lust.

Use 2: Since he [Satan] worketh by representation and promise, you must be prepared against both.

(1) As he worketh by representation of the fair show and splendid appearance of worldly things, you must check it:

(i) By considering the little substance and reality that is in this fair appearance: 'The fashion (*schema*) of this world passeth away' (1 Corinthians 7:31). It is but a draft, an empty pageantry; so it is called in Psalm 39:6, 'A vain show'; an image, shadow, or dream, that vanisheth in a trice [moment]. So Proverbs 23:5, 'Wilt thou set thine eyes upon that which is not?' It was not a while ago, and within a little while it will not be again, at least to us it will not be; we must shortly bid goodnight to all the world: 'All flesh is grass, and the glory thereof as the flower of the grass' (1 Peter 1:24). David saith in Psalm 119:86: 'I have seen an end of all perfection.' It is good often to intermingle these serious thoughts of the frailty of all sublunary [literally, 'beneath the moon'] enjoyments, to keep us modest in what we have, or desire to have, that we may not be blinded with the delusion of the flesh, and enchanted with an admiration of worldly felicity [happiness].

(ii) As the devil seeketh to open the eye of sense, so must we open the eye of faith: 'We look not at the things which are seen, but at the things which are not seen; for the things which are seen are temporal, but the things which are not seen are eternal' (2 Corinthians 4:18). Things unseen must be every day greatened [made more important] in our eyes, that all our pursuit after things seen may be subordinated to our desires of, and labour after, things unseen. There we must see the greatest reality, or else we have not the true Christian faith: 'Faith is the substance of things hoped for, and the evidence of things not seen' (Hebrews 11:1). It is such an evidence of the worth and reality of the unseen glory as draweth off the heart from things seen, which are so pleasing to the flesh. Faith sets it before the eye of the soul in the promises of the gospel: 'Who have fled for refuge to lay hold upon the hope set before us' (Hebrews 6:18). 'Who for the joy that was set before him endured the cross ...' (Hebrews 12:2).

(2) As he dealeth with us by promise. Everything we hope to get by sin is a kind of promise or offer of the devil to us; as, suppose [for example,] by unconscionable [unprincipled] dealing in our calling [actions in our daily jobs]. Here consider two things: (i) The falsity of the devil's promises; (ii) The truth and stability of God's promises.

(i) The falsity of Satan's promises. Either he giveth not what he promised, as he promised our first parents to be as gods: 'Ye shall be as gods' (Genesis 3:5); and what ensued? 'Man that is in honour and understandeth not, is like the beasts that perish' (Psalm 44:12); degraded to the beasts, as the brutish and bestial nature prevailed in him when he fell from God. Or else, if we have them, we were [would be] better without them; we have them with a curse, with the loss of better things: 'O LORD, all that forsake thee shall be ashamed, and they that depart from me shall be written in the earth' (Jeremiah 17:13). They are condemned to this felicity [poor happiness]: we have them with stings of conscience: 'I have sinned, in that I have betrayed innocent blood; and he cast down the pieces of silver in the temple, and went and hanged himself' (Matthew 27:4, 5) – which are most quick and sensible [all this will be terrible] when we come to die: 'He that getteth riches, and not by right, shall leave them in the midst of his days, and at his end shall be a fool' (Jeremiah 17:11). Now [then,] rise up in indignation against the temptation. [Say to yourself] 'Shall I sell my birthright? "Lose my fatness to rule over the trees?"' – so said the olive-tree in Jotham's parable (Judges 9:9).

(ii) The sufficiency and stability of God's promises.

First, Sufficiency: 'I am the Almighty God; walk before me, and be thou perfect' (Genesis 17:1); 'Godliness is profitable for all things, having the promise of the life that now is, and of that which is to come' (1 Timothy 4:8); – of heaven and of earth: 'Seek ye first the kingdom of God, and the righteousness thereof, and all these things shall be added to you' (Matthew 6:33). It may be you have less than those that indulge themselves in all manner of shifts and wiles, but you shall have enough, not to be left wholly destitute: 'He hath said, I will never leave thee, nor forsake thee' (Hebrews 13:5). And you shall have it with contentment: 'In the house of the righteous is much treasure, but in the revenues of the wicked is trouble' (Proverbs 15:6); and 'better is a little with righteousness, than great revenues with sin' (Proverbs 16:8). And you have it so as not to lose other things.

Secondly, Stability: 'All the promises of God in him are Yea, and in him Amen' (2 Corinthians 1:20); and 'That by two immutable things, in which it was impossible for God to lie, we might have strong consolation...' (Hebrews 6:18); 'Thy testimonies have I taken as an heritage for ever: they are the rejoicing of my heart' (Psalm 119:111).

(3) Observe [the words:] – *Fall down* – The pride of the devil: he sinneth from the beginning (1 John 3:8). The sin of pride was fatal to him at first, and the cause of those chains of darkness in which now he is held; yet still he sinneth the same sin, he requireth adoration, and would be admitted into a partnership of divine worship. He obtained it from pagans and idolaters, not from Christ. The angel deprecates and detests it: 'And I fell at his feet to worship him. And he said unto me, See thou do it not; for I am thy fellow-servant, and of thy brethren that have the testimony of Jesus: worship thou God' (Revelation 19:10). So Revelation 22:9: 'I fell down to worship before the face of the angel that showed me these things. And he said to me, See thou do it not: for I am thy fellow servant, and of thy brethren the prophets, and of them that keep the sayings of this book: worship God.' Paul, when the priests at Lycaonia were about to sacrifice to him: 'When the apostles heard of it, they rent their clothes, and ran in among the people, crying out, and saying, Sirs, why do you these things? We also are men of like passions with you, and preach unto you that ye should turn from these vanities unto the living God' (Acts 14:14, 15). But the evil angels are apt to invade the rights of God.

6

Then saith Jesus unto him, Get thee hence, Satan: for it is written, Thou shalt worship the Lord thy God, and him only shalt thou serve (Matthew 4:10).

Thirdly, Christ's answer and reply, which is double: (1) By way of rebuke, defiance, and bitter reprehension: *Get thee hence, Satan*; (2) By way of confutation: *For it is written, etc.*

(1) The rebuke showeth Christ's indignation against idolatry: 'Get thee hence, Satan'.

This was not to be endured. Twice Christ useth this form of speech, *hypage, Satana* – (a) to Satan tempting him to idolatry here, and (b) when his servant [Peter] dissuaded him from suffering: 'Get thee behind me, Satan, for thou art an offence to me; for thou savourest not the things that be of God, but those that be of men' (Matthew 16:23). This suggestion intrenched or touched upon the glory of God, the other upon his love to mankind; and Christ could endure neither; Satan is commanded out of his presence with indignation. The same zeal we see in his servants: in Moses in case of idolatry: he brake the tables (Exodus 32:19); so in case of contradiction to the faith of Christ, Paul taketh up Elymas: 'O full of subtilty and all mischief, thou child of the devil, thou enemy of all righteousness, wilt thou not cease to pervert the right ways of the Lord?' (Acts 13:10).

Open blasphemy must be abhorred, and needeth not only a confutation but a rebuke. Besides, it was an impudent demand of Satan to require adoration from him, to whom adoration is due from every creature; to ask him to bow down before him, to whom every knee must bow: and therefore a bold temptation must have a peremptory answer. There is no mincing [of words] in such cases. It is no way contrary to that lenity [mildness] that was in Christ; and it teacheth us, in such open cases of blasphemy and downright sin, not to parley with the devil, but to defy him.

(2) By way of confutation: 'For it is written, Thou shalt worship the Lord thy God, and him only shalt thou serve'. Where observe:

(i) Christ answereth to the main point, not to by-matters [less vital things]. He doth not dispute the devil's title, nor debate the reality of his promises; to do this would tacitly imply a liking of the temptation. No; but he disproveth the evil of the suggestion from this unclean and proud spirit: a better answer could not be given unto the tempter. So that herein we see the wisdom of Christ, which teacheth us to pass by impertinent [irrelevant] matters, and to speak expressly to the cause in hand in all our debates with Satan and his instruments.

(ii) He citeth scripture, and thereby teacheth that the Word of God, laid up in the heart and used pertinently, will ward off the blows of every temptation. This weapon Christ used all along with success, and therefore it is well called, 'The sword of the Spirit' (Ephesians 6:17). It is a sword, and so a weapon both offensive and defensive: 'The word of God is quick and powerful, sharper than any two-edged sword, piercing even to the dividing asunder of soul and spirit, and of the joints and marrow, and is a discerner of the thoughts and intents of the heart' (Hebrews 4:12).

And 'a sword of the Spirit', because the Spirit is the author of it: 'Holy men of God spake as they were moved by the Holy Ghost' (2 Peter 1:21). He formed and fashioned this weapon for us; and because its efficacy dependeth on the Spirit, who timeously [when the time requires it] bringeth it to our remembrance, and doth enliven the Word and maketh it effectual. Therefore it teacheth us to be much acquainted with the Lord's written Word.

The timely calling to mind of a word in scripture is better than all other arguments – a word forbidding or threatening such an evil: 'Thy word have I hid in my heart, that I might not sin against thee' (Psalm 119:11); pressing the practice of such a duty when we are slow of heart: 'Thy word hath quickened me' (Psalm 119:50); or a word speaking encouragement to the soul exercised with such a cross: 'Ye have forgotten the exhortation which speaketh unto you as unto children, My son, despise not thou the chastening of the Lord, nor faint when thou art rebuked of him' (Hebrews 12:5); 'Unless thy law had been my delight, I should then have perished in mine affliction' (Psalm 119:92); still it breaketh the strength of the temptation, whatsoever it be.

(iii) The words are cited out of the book of Deuteronomy. Indeed out of that book all Christ's answers are taken, which showeth us the excellency of that book. It was of great esteem among the Jews, and it should be so among all Christians, and it will be so of all that read it attentively. The church could not have wanted it [done without it].

(iv) The places out of which it is cited are two: Deuteronomy 6:13, 'Thou shalt fear the LORD thy God, and serve him, and swear by his name'; and again, Deuteronomy 10:20, 'Thou shalt fear the LORD thy God, and serve him, and to him shalt thou cleave [stick fast]'. Christ, according to the Septuagint[13], 'Thou shalt worship the Lord thy God, and

---

13. Septuagint: the Old Testament translation into Greek made in Egypt and complete by the second century BC.

him only shalt thou serve.' *Monoi, only*, which is emphatical, seemeth to be added to the text, but it is necessarily implied in the words of Moses; for his scope was to bind the people to the fear and worship of one God. None was so wicked and profane as to deny that God was to be feared and worshipped; but many might think that either the creatures or the gods of the Gentiles might be taken into fellowship of this reverence and adoration.

Him is *only him*; *autoi* is exclusive, if *monoi* were left out. See the place, Deuteronomy 6:13, 14, 'Thou shalt fear the LORD thy God, and serve him, and shalt swear by his name; ye shall not go after other gods, of the gods of the people which are round about you.' And in other places it is expressed; as 1 Samuel 7:3: 'If you prepare your hearts unto the LORD, and serve him only.' The devil excepts [takes objection] not against this interpretation, as being fully convinced and silenced by it. And it is a known story that this was the cause why the pagans would not admit the God of the Jews, as revealed in the Old Testament, or Christ, as revealed in the New, to be an object of adoration, because he would be worshipped alone, all other deities excluded. The gods of the heathens were good-fellow gods, would admit partnership; as common whores [prostitutes] are less jealous than the married wife: though their lovers went to never so many besides themselves, yet to them it was all one, whensoever they returned to them and brought their gifts and offerings.

(v) In this place quoted by our Saviour there is employed a distinction of inward and outward worship. *Fear* is for inward worship, *serve* is for outward worship, and the profession of the same. *Fear* in Moses is expounded *worship* by Christ; so Matthew 15:9, compared with Isaiah

29:13, 'In vain do they worship me, teaching for doctrines the commandments of men'; but in the prophet it is 'Their fear towards me is taught by the precepts of men.' He that worshippeth feareth and reverenceth what he worshippeth, or else all his worship is but a compliment and empty formality. So that the *fear* of God is that reverence and estimation that we have of God, the *serving* of God is the necessary effect and fruit of it; for service is an open testimony of our reverence and worship. In this place you have *worship* and *service*, both which are due to God only. But that you may perceive the force of our Saviour's argument, and also of this precept, I shall a little dilate [enlarge] on the word *service*, what the scripture intendeth thereby.

Satan saith, 'Bow down and worship me': Christ saith, 'Thou shalt worship the Lord thy God, and him only shalt thou serve.' Under *service*, prayer and thanksgiving is comprehended: 'And the residue thereof he maketh a god, even his graven image: he falleth down unto it, and worshippeth it, and prayeth unto it, and saith, Deliver me, for thou art my god' (Isaiah 44:17). This is one of the external acts whereby the idolater showeth the esteem of his heart; so Jeremiah 2:27: 'Saying to a stock, Thou art my father; and to a stone, Thou hast brought me forth.'

So, under *serving*, sacrifice is comprehended: 'Ye shall not fear other gods, nor bow yourselves to them, nor serve them, nor sacrifice to them' (2 Kings 17:35). Again, burning of incense: 'My people have forgotten me, they have burnt incense to vanity' (Jeremiah 18:15). Preaching for them; 'The pastors also have transgressed against me, and the prophets prophesied by Baal' (Jeremiah 2:8). Asking counsel of them: 'My people ask counsel at their stocks, and their staff declareth unto them; for the spirit of whoredoms hath caused them to err, and they have gone a whoring from under their God' (Hosea 4:12). So building temples, altars, or other monuments unto them: 'Israel hath forgotten his Maker, and buildeth temples' (Hosea 8:14); and 7:11, 'Their altars are as heaps in the furrows of the fields.' Erecting of ministries, or doing any ministerial work for their honour: 'Ye have borne the tabernacle of your Moloch and Chiun your images the star of your god, which ye made to yourselves' (Amos 5:26), as God appointed the Levites to bear the tabernacle for communion in the service of them. 'Are not they that eat of the sacrifices partakers of the altar?' (1 Corinthians 10:18); 'Ye cannot drink the cup of the Lord and the cup of the devils; ye cannot be partakers of the Lord's table and of the table of devils' (verse 21). So 2 Corinthians 6:16, 17, 'What agreement hath the temple of God with idols?'

In short, for it is endless to reckon up all which the scripture comprehendeth under service and gestures of reverence: 'Thou shalt not bow down thyself to them, nor serve them' (Exodus 20:5). Bowing the knee: 'I have left me seven thousand in Israel, which have not bowed the knee to Baal' (1 Kings 19:18). Kissing them: 'They kiss the calves' (Hosea 13:18). Lifting up the eyes: 'He hath not lift up his eyes to the idols of the house of Israel' (Ezekiel 18:6). Stretching out the hand: 'If we have stretched our hands to a strange God' (Psalm 44:20).

So that you see all gestures of reverence are forbidden as terminated to idols. Thus strict and jealous is God in his law, that we might not bow down and worship the devil, or anything that is set up by him.

Doctrine: That religious service and religious worship is due to God only, and not to be given to saint, or angel, or any creature.

Thus Christ defeateth the devil's temptation, and thus should we be under the awe of God's authority, that we may not yield to the like temptation when the greatest advantages imaginable are offered to us. Here I shall show: (1) What is worship, and the kinds of it; (2) I shall prove that worship is due to God; (3) Not only worship, but service; (4) That both are due to God alone.

1. What is worship?
In the general it implieth these three things: an act of the judgment, apprehending an excellency in the object worshipped; an act of the will, or a readiness to yield to it, suitably to the degree of excellency which we apprehend in it; and an external act of the body whereby it is expressed. This is the general nature of worship, common to all the sorts of it.

The kinds of it. Now worship is of two kinds: civil and religious. Religious worship is a special duty due to God, and commanded in the first table. Civil honour and worship is commanded in the second table. They are expressed by 'godliness and righteousness' (1 Timothy 6:11), and 'godliness and honesty' (1 Timothy 2:2).

(1) *For religious worship*
There is a twofold religious worship. One when we are right for the object, and do only worship the true God; this is required in the first commandment. The other when we are right for the means, when we worship the true God by such means as he hath appointed, not by an image, idol, or outward representation.

Opposite to this there is an evil idolatrous sinful worship, when that which is due to the Creator is given to any creature; which is primary or secondary. Primary, when the image or idol is accounted God, or worshipped as such, as the sottish [foolish] heathens do. Or secondary, when the images themselves are not worshipped as having any godhead properly in themselves, but as they relate to, represent, or are made use of, in the worship of him who is accounted God. We shall find this done by the wiser heathens, worshipping their images, not as gods themselves, but as intending to worship their gods in these and by these. So also among some who would be called Christians. Thus the representing the true God by images is condemned: 'Take ye good heed unto yourselves, for ye saw no manner of similitude on the day that the LORD spake unto you in Horeb, out of the midst of the fire, lest ye corrupt yourselves, and make you a graven image, the similitude of any figure, the likeness of male or female' (Deuteronomy 4:15-17).

Again, sinful worship is twofold: more gross of idols, representing false gods, called worshipping of devils; or more subtle, when worship is given to saints or holy men: 'As Peter was coming in, Cornelius met him, and fell down at this feet, and worshipped him. But Peter took him up, saying, Stand up, I myself also am a man' (Acts 10:25, 26); 'Paul and Barnabas, when they heard this, rent their clothes, and ran in among the people, crying out and saying, Sirs, why do you these things? We also are men of like passions with you ...' (Acts 14:14, 15). Or to angels: 'When John fell at the angel's feet to worship him, he said, See thou do it not: for I am thy fellow-servant, and of thy brethren the prophets' (Revelation 22:8).

(2) *Civil worship is when we give men and angels due reverence*, and:

(i) With respect to their stations [status] and relations, whatever their qualifications be, as to magistrates, ministers, parents, great men; we are to reverence and honour them according to their degree and quality: according to the fifth commandment, 'Honour thy father and thy mother'; and to 'esteem them very highly in love for their work's sake' (1 Thessalonians 5:13). Or:

(ii) A reverential worshipping or esteeming them for their qualifications of wisdom and holiness: good men had 'favour with all the people' (Acts 2:47). Such respect living saints get, such angels may have when they appear: Abraham 'bowed himself towards the ground' (Genesis 18:2): and in Genesis 19:1, Lot 'rose up to meet them, and bowed himself with his face towards the ground'.

Now, whether the worship be civil or religious may be gathered by the circumstances thereof; as if the act, end, or other circumstances be religious, the action or worship itself must be so also. It is one thing to bow the knee in salutation, another thing to bow in prayer before an image.

2. That worship is due to God

These two notions live and die together, that God is, and that he ought to be worshipped. It appeareth by our Saviour's reasoning: 'God is a spirit, and they that worship him must worship him in spirit and in truth' (John 4:24). He giveth directions about the manner of worship, but supposeth it [assumes] that he will be worshipped. When God had proclaimed his name and manifested himself to Moses, 'Moses made haste, and bowed himself and worshipped' (Exodus 34:8).

It is the crime charged upon the Gentiles, that 'when they knew God, they glorified him not as God' (Romans 1:21). They knew a divine power, but did not give him a worship at least competent to his nature. God pleadeth his right: 'If I be a father, where is mine honour? If I be a master, where is my fear?' (Malachi 1:6). And God, who is the common parent and absolute master of all, must have both a worship and honour, in which reverence and fear is mixed with love and joy; so that if God be, worship is certainly due to him.

They that have no worship are as if they had no God. The psalmist proveth atheism by that: 'The fool hath said in his heart, There is no God' (Psalm 14:1); and verse 4: 'They call not upon God.' The acknowledgement of a king doth imply subjection to his laws; so doth the acknowledgement of his God imply a necessity of worshipping him.

3. That both worship and service is due to God: 'Him shalt thou worship, and him shalt thou serve.'

The worship of God is both internal and external; the internal consisteth in that love and reverence which we owe to him; the external, in those offices and duties by which our honour and respect to God is signified and expressed: both are necessary, both believing with the heart, and confession with the mouth: 'If thou shalt confess with thy mouth the Lord Jesus, and shalt believe in thy heart that God raised him from the dead, thou shalt be saved. For with the heart man believeth unto righteousness, and with the mouth confession is made unto salvation' (Romans 10:9, 10). The soul and life of our worship and godliness lieth in our faith, love, reverence and delight in God above all other things; the visible expression of it is in invocation, thanksgiving, prayers, and sacraments, and other acts of outward worship.

Now, it is not enough that we own God with the heart, but we must own him with the body also. In the heart: 'Serve the LORD with fear, and rejoice with trembling' (Psalm 2:11). Such as will become the greatness and goodness of God, with outward and bodily worship must now own him in all those prescribed duties in which these affections are acted [expressed]. The spirit must be in it, and the body also.

There are two extremes. Some confine all their respect to God to bodily worship and external forms: 'This people draweth nigh unto me with their mouth, and honoureth me with their lips; but their hearts are far from me' (Matthew 16:8). They use the external rites of worship, but their affections are no way suited to the God whom they worship: it is the heart that must be the principal and chief agent in the business, without which it is but the carcase of a duty, without the life and the soul. The other extreme is, that we are not called to an external bodily worship under the gospel. Why did he then appoint the ordinances of preaching, prayer, singing of psalms, baptism and the Lord's supper? God, that made the whole man, body and soul, must be worshipped of the whole man. Therefore, besides the inward affections, there must be external actions, whereby we express our respect and reverence to God.

4. That both these, religious worship and service, are due to God alone. I prove it by these arguments:

(1) Those things which are due to God as God are due to him alone, and no creature, without sacrilege, can claim any part and fellowship in that worship and adoration, neither can it be given to any creature without idolatry. But now religious worship and service is due to God as God: 'He is thy Lord,

and worship thou him' (Psalm 45:11). Our worship and service is due to him, not only for his super-eminent excellency, but because of our creation, preservation and redemption. Therefore we must worship and serve him, and him only: 'I am the LORD; that is my name: and my glory will I not give to another, nor my praise to graven images' (Isaiah 42:8). God challengeth it as Jehovah, the great self-being, from whom we have received life and breath, and all things. This glory God will not suffer to be given to another. And therefore the apostle showeth the wretched estate of the Galatians: 'When ye knew not God, ye did service to them that by nature are no gods' (4:8); that is, they worshipped for gods those things which really were no gods. There is no kind of religious worship or service, under any name whatsoever, to be given to any creature, but to God only; for what is due to the Creator as Creator cannot be given to the creature.

(2) The nature of religious worship is such, that it cannot be terminated on [directed to] any object but God; for it is a profession of our dependence and subjection. Now, whatever invisible power this worship is tendered unto [offered to] must be omniscient, omnipresent, omnipotent.

Omniscient, who knows the thoughts, cogitations [mental processes], secret purposes of our heart, which God alone doth: 'Give unto every one according to his ways, whose heart thou knowest; for thou, even thou only, knowest the hearts of all the children of men' (1 Kings 8:39). It is God's prerogative to know the inward motions and thoughts of the heart, whether they be sincere or no in their professions of dependence and subjection.

So *omnipresent*, that he may be ready at hand to help us

and relieve us: 'Am I a God at hand, and not a God afar off? Can any hide himself in secret places, that I shall not see him? saith the LORD. Do not I fill heaven and earth? saith the LORD' (Jeremiah 23:23, 24). The palace of heaven doth not so confine him and enclose him but that he is present everywhere by his essential presence, and powerful and efficacious providence.

Besides *omnipotent*: 'I will cry unto God most high, unto God who performeth all things for me' (Psalm 57:2). Alas! what a cold formality were [would be] prayer if we should speak to those that know us not, and who are not near to help us, or have no sufficiency of power to help us! Therefore these professions of dependence and subjection must be made to God alone.

(3) To give religious worship to the creatures, is without command, without promise, and without examples, and therefore without any faith in [the heart of] the worshipper, or acceptance of God [on God's part]. Where is there any command or direction, or approved example, of this in scripture? God will accept only what he commanded, and without a promise it will be unprofitable to us: and it is a superstitious innovation of our own to devise any religious worship for which there is no example at all whereby it may be recommended to us. Certainly no action can be commended to us as godly which is not prescribed of [by] God, by whose Word and institution every action is sanctified which otherwise would be common; and no action can be profitable to us which God hath not promised to accept, or hath accepted from his people. But giving religious worship to a creature is of this nature.

(4) It is against the express command of God, the threatening of scripture, and the examples recorded in the Word. Against the express command of God – both the first and second commandments, the one respecting the object, the other the means; that we must not serve other gods, nor go after them, nor bow down unto them. It is against the threatenings of the Word in all those places where God is said to be 'a jealous God'. God is said to 'put on jealousy as a cloak' (Isaiah 59:17; that is, the upper and outmost garment. He will be known and plainly profess himself to be so). So Exodus 34:14: 'The LORD, whose name is Jealous, is a jealous God'. Things are distinguished from the same kind by their names, as from different kinds by their natures. Now, from the *legomenoi theoi* ['called gods'], God will be distinguished by his jealousy, that he will not endure any partners in his worship. It is against examples: 'When I had heard and seen, I fell down to worship before the feet of the angel which showed me these things. And he said unto me, See thou do it not', etc. The argument is, 'I am thy fellow-servant, and of thy brethren the prophets, and of them which keep the saying of this book: worship God' (Revelation 19:10; 22:8).

Uses
Use 1: To condemn those who do not make conscience of the worship of God. There are an irreligious sort of men that never call upon him, in public or in private, in the family or in the closet; but wholly forget the God that made them, at whose expense they are maintained and kept. Wherefore had you reasonable souls, but to praise, honour and glorify your Creator? Surely if God be your God, that is, your Creator and preserver, the duty will presently fall upon you:

'Thou shalt worship the Lord thy God.' If you believe there is a God, why do not you call upon him? The neglect of his worship argueth doubting thoughts of his being; for if there be such a supreme Lord, to whom one day you must give an account, how dare you live without him in the world?

All the creatures glorify him passively, but you have a heart and a tongue to glorify him actually. Man is the mouth of the creation, to return to God the praise of all that wisdom, goodness and power which is seen in the things that are made. Now you should make one among the worshippers of God. A heathen could say, *Si essem luscinia*, [If I were a nightingale ...] etc. Are you a Christian, and have such advantages to know more of God, and will you be dumb and tongue-tied in his praises?

Use 2: To condemn the idolatry of the Papists. Synesius[14] said that the devil is *eidolochares*, that he rejoiceth in idols. Here we see what was the upshot of his temptations, even to bring men to worship and bow down before something that is not God. Herein he was gratified by the heathen nations, and no less by the Papists. Witness their worshipping of images, their invocation of the Virgin Mary and other saints, the adoring before the bread in the Eucharist, etc. I know they have many evasions; but yet the stain of idolatry sticketh so close to them, that all the water in the sea will not wash them clean from it. This text clearly stareth them in the face, 'Thou shalt worship the Lord thy God, and him only shalt thou serve.' Not saints, not angels, not images, etc. They say, Moses only said, and Christ repeateth it from him, 'Thou shalt worship the Lord thy God'; but not *only*, so that

---

14. Synesius: a bishop of the Early Church who died about AD 414.

the last clause is restrictive, not the first, but some worship may be given to the creature. Civil, we grant, but not religious; and worship is the most important word. They distinguish of [between] *latreia* and *douleia*. The devil demanded of Christ only *proskynesai*, 'fall down and worship me'; not as the supreme author of all God's gifts, but as subordinate: 'all these things are delivered unto me'.

But then Christ's words were not apposite [suitable] to refute the tempter's impudency. Besides, for the distinction of *douleia* and *latreia*, the words are promiscuously used; so their distinction of absolute and relative worship; besides that they are groundless, they are unknown to the vulgar, who promiscuously give worship to God, saints, images, relics. Some of the learned of them have confessed this abuse, and bewailed it.

Espencaeus, a Sorbonnist[15] said:

> 'Are they well and godly brought up, who, being children of an hundred year old, that is, ancient Christians, do no less attribute to the saints, and trust in them, than to God himself, and that God himself is harder to be pleased, and entreated than they?'

So [similarly] George Cassander[16] [could say]:

> 'This false, pernicious opinion is too well known to have prevailed among the vulgar, while wicked men, persevering in their naughtiness, are persuaded that only by the intercession of the saints whom they have chosen to be their patrons, and worship with cold and profane ceremonies, they have pardon and grace prepared them with God; which pernicious opinion, as much as was possible, hath been confirmed by them by lying

---

15. Evidently a Roman Catholic writer who taught at the Sorbonne in Paris.
16. George Cassander: sixteenth-century Roman Catholic theologian.

miracles. And other men, not so evil, have chosen certain saints to be their patrons and helpers, have put more confidence in their merits and intercession than in the merits of Christ, and have substituted into his place the saints and Virgin mother.'

Ludovicus Vives[17] said:

'There are many Christians which [who] worship saints, both men and women, no otherwise than they worship God; and I cannot see any difference between the opinion they had of their saints, and that the Gentiles had of their gods.'

Thus far he [could go], and yet Rome [the Roman Catholic Church] will not be purged [reformed of its errors in worship].

Use 3: Use is to exhort us to worship and serve the Lord our God, and him only.

(i) Let us worship him. Worship hath its rise and foundation in the heart of the worshipper, and especially religious worship, which is given to the all-knowing God. Therefore there must we begin; we must have high thoughts, and an high esteem of God. Worship in the heart is most seen in two things – love and trust.

Love: 'Thou shalt love the LORD thy God with all thy heart, and with all thy soul, and with all thy might' (Deuteronomy 6:5). We worship God when we give him such a love as is superlative and transcendental, far above the love that we give to any other thing, that so our respect to other things may give way to our respect to God.

The other affection whereby we express our esteem of God is *trust*. This is another foundation of worship: 'Trust

---

17. Ludovicus Vives: sixteenth-century Roman Catholic theologian who taught for a time at Oxford.

in the him at all times, pour out your hearts before him' (Psalm 62:8). Well, then, inward worship lieth in these two things – delightful adhesion to God, and an entire dependence upon him. Without this worship of God we cannot keep up our service to him. Not without delight, witness these scriptures: 'Will he delight himself in the Almighty? Will he always call upon God?' (Job 27:10); 'But thou hast not called upon me, O Jacob; but thou hast been weary of me, O Israel!' (Isaiah 43:22). They that love God, and delight in him, cannot be long out of his company, they will seek all occasions to meet with God, as Jonathan and David whose souls were knit to each other. So for dependence and trust, it keepeth up service, for they that will not trust God cannot be long true to him: 'Take heed lest there be in any of you an evil heart of unbelief in departing from the living God' (Hebrews 3:12).

They that distrust God's promises will not long hold out in God's way, for dependence begets observance. When we look for all from him, we will often come to him, and take all out of his hands, and be careful how we offend him and displease him. What maketh the Christian to be so sedulous [diligent] and diligent in duties of worship? So awful and observant of God? His all cometh from God, both in life natural and spiritual. In life natural:

> The eyes of all things wait on thee, and thou givest them their food in due season. Thou openest thy hand, and satisfiest the desire of every living thing.... The LORD is nigh unto all them that call upon him, to all that call upon him in truth. He will fulfil the desire of them that fear him: he will hear their cry and will save them. The LORD preserveth all them that love him' (Psalm 145:15-20) –

implying that because their eyes are to him, the author of all their blessings, therefore they call upon him and cry to him.

(ii) Serve him. That implieth external reverence and worship. Now we are said to serve him, either with respect unto the duties which are more directly to be performed unto God, or with respect to our whole conversation [lifestyle].

[1] With respect unto the duties which are more directly to be performed unto God, such as the Word, prayer, praise, thanksgiving, sacraments, surely these must be attended upon, because they are acts of love to God, and trust in God; and these holy duties are the ways of God, wherein he hath promised to meet with his people, and hath appointed us to expect his grace, and therefore they must not be neglected by us. Therefore serve him in these things; for 'With what measure ye mete, it shall be measured to you' (Mark 4:24). It is a rule of commerce [fellowship] between us and God.

[2] In your whole conversation: 'That we might serve him without fear, in holiness and righteousness before him, all the days of our life' (Luke 1:74, 75). A Christian's conversation [lifestyle] is a continual act of worship; he ever behaveth himself as before God, doing all things, whether they be directed to God or men, out of love to God, and fear of God, and so turneth second table duties into first table duties. 'Pure religion and undefiled, before God and the Father, is this, to visit the fatherless and the widows in their affliction, and to keep himself unspotted from the world' (James 1:27); 'Submitting yourselves one to another in the fear of God' (Ephesians 5:21); and in the next verse, 'Wives, submit yourselves unto your own husbands, as unto the Lord.' So alms are a sacrifice: 'But to do good and to communicate, forget not; for with such sacrifices God is well pleased' (Hebrews 13:16).

[3] Worship and serve God so as it may look like worship and service performed to God, and due to God only, because of his nature and attributes. His nature: 'God is a Spirit, and they that worship him must worship him in spirit and in truth' (John 4:24). When hearts wander, and affections do not answer expressions, is this like worship and service done to an all-seeing Spirit? His attributes: Greatness, goodness, holiness:

(1) His greatness and glorious majesty: 'Let us serve him acceptably, with reverence and godly fear' (Hebrews 12:28). Then is there a stamp of God's majesty on the duty.

(2) His goodness and fatherly love: 'Serve the LORD with gladness, and come before his presence with singing' (Psalm 100:2).

(3) His holiness: 'I thank God, whom I serve from my forefathers, with pure conscience' (2 Timothy 1:3); 'With them that call on the Lord out of a pure heart' (2 Timothy 2:22).

7

*Then the devil leaveth him, and behold angels came and ministered unto him (*Matthew 4:11*).*

In these words you have the issue and close of Christ's temptations. The issue is double: (1) In respect of the adversary: *then the devil leaveth him.* (2) In respect of Christ himself: *behold angels came and ministered unto him.* I shall consider in both the history and the observations.

1. The history of it, as it properly belongeth to Christ: and there:

1. Of the first branch, *the recess [departure] of Satan*: 'Then the devil leaveth him.'

(1) It was necessary to be known that Christ had power to chase away the devil at his pleasure; that, as he was an instance of temptations, so he might be to us a pattern of victory and conquest. If Satan had continued tempting, this would have been obscured, which would have been an infringement of comfort to us. The devil being overcome by Christ, he may be also overcome by us Christians: 'He that is begotten of God keepeth himself, and the wicked one touched him not' (1 John 5:18). That is, he useth all care and diligence to keep himself pure, that the devil draw him not into the sin unto death, and those deliberate, scandalous sins which lead to it. Christ having overcome Satan, in our name and nature, showeth us the way how to fight against him and overcome him.

and nature, showeth us the way how to fight against him and overcome him.

(2) Christ had a work to do in the valley [Galilee (?)], and therefore was not always to be detained by temptations in the wilderness. The Spirit, that led him thither to be tempted, led him back again into Galilee to preach the gospel: 'Jesus returned in the power of the Spirit into Galilee' (Luke 4:14). All things are timed and ordered by God, and he limiteth Satan how far and how long he shall tempt.

(3) In Luke 4:13 it is said: 'He departed from him, *achri chronou*, for a season.' He never tempted him again in this solemn way hand to hand; but either abusing the simplicity of his own disciple: 'Then Peter took him, and began to rebuke him, saying, Be it far from thee, Lord; this shall not be unto thee. But he turned and said unto Peter, Get thee behind me Satan! thou art an offence unto me' (Matthew 16:22, 23); or else by his instruments, laying plots to take away his life; as often, but especially in his passion: 'This is your hour, and the power of darkness' (Luke 22:53). So John 14:30: 'The prince of this world cometh, and hath nothing in me.' Satan shall join with the Jews to destroy me, and they shall find nothing to lay to my charge; nor, indeed, have they power to do me any hurt, but that, in obedience to my Father's will, I mean voluntarily to lay down my life for sinners. So he had a permitted power over him, and was the prime instrumental cause of his sufferings; set aside his voluntary condescension to be a ransom for sinners, Satan had not any power over him, or challenge against him. Well, then, though he lost his victory, he retained his malice.

Sermon 7

2. The second branch, *the access [approach] of the good angels*: 'And behold the angels came and ministered to him.' There observe three things:

(1) The note of attention: *behold*. The Holy Ghost would excite our minds, and have us mark this: the angels are always at hand to serve Christ, but now they come to him in some singular manner – some notable appearance there was of them, probably in a visible form and shape; and so they presented themselves before the Lord to minister to him, as the devil set himself before him to molest [annoy] and vex him. As Christ's humiliation and human nature was to be manifested by the devil's coming to him and tempting assaults, so the honour of his divine nature by the ministry of angels, lest his temptations should seem to derogate [take away] from his glory. When we read the story of his temptations, how he was tempted in all parts like us, we might seem to take scandal, as if he were a mere man; therefore his humiliation is counterbalanced with the special honour done to him: he was tempted as man, but, as God, ministered unto by angels.

(2) Why did they not come before the devil was departed? I answer:

(i) Partly to show that Christ had no help but his own when he grappled with Satan. When the temptations were ended, then the good angels came, lest the victory should seem to be gotten by their help and assistance. They were admitted to the triumph, but they were not admitted to the fight: they were spectators only in the conflict (for the battle was certainly fought before God and angels) but partners in the triumph: they went away to give place to the combat, but they came visibly to congratulate the conqueror after the battle was fought and the victory gotten. Our Lord would alone foil the devil, and, when that was done, the angels came and ministered unto him.

(ii) Partly to show us that the going of the one is the coming of the other. When the devil is gone, the angels come. Certainly it is true on the contrary: 'The spirit of the LORD departed from Saul, and an evil spirit from the LORD troubled him' (1 Samuel 16:14); and it is true in this sense, if we entertain the temptation, we banish the good angels from us; there is no place for the good angels till the tempter be repulsed.

(3) Why now, and to what end, was this ministry?

(i) To put honour on the Redeemer, who is the head and lord of the angels: 'He hath set him at his own right hand in the heavenly places, far above all principalities and powers ... and gave him to be the head over all things to the church' (Ephesians 1:20, 21). So 1 Peter 3:22: 'Who is gone into heaven, and is on the right hand of God; angels, and authorities, and powers, being made subject to him.' Christ, not only as God, but as mediator, hath all of them subject to him: 'And unto the Son he saith, Let all the angels of God worship him' (Hebrews 1:6). They, as subjects and servants, are bound to obey him.

Therefore, on all occasions they attend on Christ; at his birth: 'A multitude of the heavenly host praised God, saying, Glory be to God on high, on earth peace, good will towards men' (Luke 2:13, 14). Now, in his temptations, 'The angels came and ministered unto him.' At his passion: 'There appeared to him an angel from heaven, strengthening him' (Luke 22:43). At his resurrection, 'An angel rolled away the stone from the grave', and attested the truth of it (Matthew 28:2). At his ascension, the angels declared the manner of his going to heaven, and return to judgement (Acts 1:10, 11). So now they came to attend Christ, as subjects of their prince, to tender their service and homage to him, and receive his commands.

(ii) For his consolation, inward and outward.

First, Inward, as messengers sent from God; and so their coming was a token of God's special love and favour to him, and care over him. The devil had mentioned in one of his temptations, 'He shall give his angels charge over thee.' This is a truth, and in due time to be verified; not at Satan's instance, but when God pleased. Therefore it was a comfort to Christ to have solemn messengers sent from heaven to applaud his triumph.

Secondly, Outward, they were sent to serve him, either to convey him back from the mountain, where Satan had set him, or to bring him food, as they did to Elijah: 'And as he lay and slept under a juniper-tree, behold an angel touched him, and said unto him, Arise and eat. And he looked, and behold there was a cake baken on the coals, and a cruse of water at his head: and he did eat and drink, and laid him down again (1 Kings 19:5, 6).

Diakonein, the word here used, is often taken in that sense in the New Testament: 'She arose and ministered unto them' (Matthew 8:15), that is, served them at meat; 'When saw we thee an hungered ... and did not minister unto thee?' (Matthew 25:44). The name of *deacons* is derived hence as they 'served tables' or provided meat for the poor (Acts 6:2). So Luke 10:40: 'My sister hath left me, *diakonein*, to serve alone', meaning, to prepare provisions for the family; so Luke 17:8: 'Gird thyself and serve me', that is, at the table;

again, Luke 22:27: 'Whether is greater, he that sits at meat, or he that serveth?' or ministereth. So John 12:2: 'They made a supper, and Martha served, but Lazarus was one of those that sat at the table with him.'

Thus the angels ministered unto Christ. This sort of ministry agreeth with what was said of his hunger, which was the occasion of Satan's temptations.

2. Observations
As Christ is a pattern of all those providences which are dispensed to the people of God.

Doctrine 1. That the days of God's people's conflicts and trials will not always last.

There are alternative changes and vicissitudes [ups and downs] in their condition upon earth; sometimes they are vexed with the coming of the tempter, and then encouraged and cheered by the presence of angels; after storms come days of joy and gladness – 'the devil departeth, and the angels came and ministered to him.' So Psalm 34:19, 'Many are the afflictions of the righteous, but the LORD delivereth him out of them all.' Here is their present conflict and their final conquest. Look on a Christian on his dark side, and there are afflictions, and afflictions many for number and kind; look on his luminous part [bright side], and there is the Lord to take care of him, to deliver him, and the deliverance is complete: 'the LORD delivereth him out of them all.' God will put an end to their conflict sooner or later; sometimes visibly in this life, or if he doth not deliver them till death, or from death, he will deliver them by death; then he delivereth them from all sin and misery at once, for death is theirs. The reasons are these:

Sermon 7

1. *God considereth what will become [be appropriate to] himself, his pity and fidelity.*

(1) God's own pity and mercy: 'Ye have heard of the patience of Job, and have seen the end of the Lord, that the Lord is very pitiful, and of tender mercy' (James 5:11). God will give an happy end to our conflicts and trials, as he did to Job, that he may be known to be a God pitiful and merciful: Job is set up as a public visible instance and monument of God's tender mercy. We must not measure our afflictions by the smart [pain of them], but the end of them; what the merciful God will do at length: the beginning is from Satan, but the end from the Lord. If we look to the beginning, we draw an ill [false] picture of God in our minds, as if he were harsh, severe, and cruel to his creatures, yea, to his best servants; but in the end we find him very tender of his people, and that sense hath made lies of God. At the very time when we think God hath forgotten us, he is ready to hear and to remove the trouble. 'I said in my haste, I am cut off; nevertheless, thou heardest the voice of my supplications' (Psalm 31:22). The Son of God was hungry, transported and carried to and fro by the devil, from the pinnacle of the temple to a high mountain, tempted by a blasphemous suggestion to fall down and worship the impure spirit; but at length 'the devil leaveth him, and the angels came and ministered to him'.

(2) God's fidelity, which will not permit him to suffer you to be tempted above measure. We do not stand to the devil's courtesy, to tempt us as long as he list, but are in the hands of the faithful God: 'There hath no temptation taken you but what is common to man: but God is faithful, who will not suffer you to be tempted above that ye are able; but will with the temptation also make a way to escape, that ye

may be able to bear it' (1 Corinthians 10:13). What a heap of consolations are there in that one place, as

(i) That temptations are but ordinary and to be looked for: there is no *peirasmos* [temptation], but it is *anthropinos*, *incident to human nature*; it hath nothing extraordinary in it. If the Son of God in human nature was not exempted, why should we expect a privilege apart to ourselves, not common to others?

(ii) That God's conduct is gentle; he inflicteth nothing and permitteth nothing to be inflicted upon you beyond measure, and above strength; but, as Jacob drove as the little ones were able to bear, so God proportioneth trials to our strength. Before you have final deliverance, you shall have present support.

(iii) That he will, together with the temptation, give *ekbasin*, *a passage out*, a way to escape. And all this is assured to us by his faithfulness; the conflict shall be tolerable when it is at the highest, and the end comfortable. God doth bridle the malice and hatred of Satan and his instruments; he hath taken an obligation upon himself to do so, that he may omit no part of his care towards us. A good man will not overburden his beast.

2. *The Lord considereth also our frailty, both with respect to natural and spiritual strength.*

(1) Natural strength. The Psalmist telleth us that 'he will not always chide, and keep his anger for ever' (Psalm 103:9). Why? One reason is that 'he knoweth our frame, and remembereth we are dust' (verse 14). He may express his just displeasure, and correct us for our sins for a while; but he taketh off his punishing hand again, because he knoweth we are soon apt to faint and fail, being but a little enlivened

dust, of a weak constitution, not able to endure long troubles and vexations. Job pleadeth: 'Is my strength the strength of stones? Or is my flesh of brass?' (Job 6:12). We have not strength to subsist [go on and on] under perpetual troubles, but are soon broken and subdued by them.

(2) With respect to spiritual strength, the best are subject to great infirmities, which oft betray us to sin, if our vexations be great and long: 'The rod of the wicked shall not rest on the lot of the righteous, lest the righteous put forth their hands to iniquity' (Psalm 125:3). The oppressions of wicked men shall not be so lasting and durable as that the temptations should be of too great force; this might shake the constancy of the best. He knoweth nothing in divinity that knoweth not that God worketh congruously [appropriately], and attempereth [matches] his providence to our strength, and so will not only give an increase of internal grace, but lessen and abate the outward temptation; that his external government conduceth to the preservation of the saints, as well as his internal, by supporting their spirits with more liberal aids of grace. Therefore God will cause the temptation to cease when it is overpressing. But all must be left to his wisdom and holy methods.

3. *With respect to the devil and his instruments, to whose malice he sets bounds, [and] who otherwise would know no measure.*

(1) For *the devil*, see Revelation 2:10: 'Fear none of those things which thou shalt suffer. Behold! The devil shall cast some of you into prison, that you may be tried; and ye shall have tribulation ten days.' Mark [see] how they are comforted against the persecution coming upon them: Partly because the cause was clearly God's, for all this trouble was

by the instigation of the devil, making use of his instruments (Ephesians 2:2, he is called 'the prince of the power of the air, the spirit that worketh in the children of disobedience'); partly because the persecution raised would not be universal – 'some of you', not 'all' – and those not persecuted unto the death, but only cast into prison; partly from the end [in view] that they should be tried. It was not penal or castigatory, but probatory. The devil would destroy you, but God would suffer you only to be tried, so that they should come forth like the three children out of the furnace, without singeing of their garments, or like Daniel out of the lions' den, without a scratch or maim, or as Christ here. The devil got not one jot of ground upon him [no advantage over Christ]. Partly [too, it was] from the duration, ten days – that is, in prophetical account, ten years, reckoning each day for a year (Numbers 14:34). It was not long; the saddest [most trying] afflictions will have an end. All which showeth how God bridleth and moderateth the rage of Satan, and his evil influence.

(2) For *his instruments*, God saith in Zechariah 1:15: 'I am very sorely displeased with the heathen that were at ease; for I was but a little displeased, and they helped forward the affliction.' The instruments of God's chastisements lay on without mercy, and being of cruel minds and destructive intentions, which are heightened in them by Satan, are severe executioners of God's wrath; and if God did not restrain them by the invisible chains of his providence, we should never see good day more. Well, then, you see the reasons why the children of God, though they have many troubles and conflicts, yet they are not everlasting troubles.

Use of instruction to the people of God

It teacheth them three lessons: comfort, patience, obedience.

(1) *Comfort and encouragement* to them that are under a gloomy day. This will not always last. He may try you for a while, and you may be under great conflicts, and wants, and difficulties, as he tried the woman of Canaan with discouraging answers. But at last [he said], 'Woman, great is thy faith, be it unto thee even as thou wilt' (Matthew 15:28). He tried his disciples when he meant to feed the multitude: 'Whence shall we buy bread that all these may eat? This he said to prove them, for he himself knew what he would do' (John 6:5, 6).

A poor believer is tried, children increase, trading grows dead [money is scarce] in hard times; how shall so many mouths be filled? He promiseth Abraham a numerous posterity, but for a great while he goeth childless. God promiseth David a kingdom, yet for a while he is fain to [disposed to] shift [resort to expedients] for his life, and skulk up and down in the wilderness. He intended to turn water into wine, but first all the store must be spent. He meaneth to revive the hearts of his contrite ones, but for a while they lie under great doubts and fears. Moses' hand must be made leprous before it wrought miracles. Jesus loved Lazarus, and meant to recover him, but he must be dead first. But I must not run too far.

There will be tedious conflicts and trials, but yet there is hope of deliverance: God is willing and God is able. He is willing, because he is sufficiently inclined to it by the grace and favour that he beareth his people: 'The LORD taketh pleasure in his people; he will beautify the meek with salvation' (Psalm 149:4). The Lord loveth their persons, and he loveth their prosperity and happiness: 'He hath pleasure in the prosperity of his servants' (Psalm 35:27). God is able either as to [both in view of his] wisdom or power: *wisdom*: 'The Lord knoweth how to deliver the godly out of temptation' (2 Peter 2:7). Many times we know not which way, but God knoweth; he is never at a loss. Then for his *power*: power hath a twofold notion, of authority and might. He hath authority enough. The sovereign dominion of God is a great prop to our faith. All things in the world are at his disposal to use them for his own glory: 'Command deliverances for Jacob' (Psalm 44:4). Angels, devils, men, the hearts of the greatest men, are all at his command. He hath might and strength: 'Our God, whom we serve, is able to deliver us' (Daniel 3:17), and what then can let [stand in our way]?

(2) *Patience*: we must be contented, with the Son of God, to tarry [await] his leisure, and undergo our course of trial, as Christ patiently continued, till enough was done to instruct the Church: 'He that believeth will not make haste' (Isaiah 28:16). The people of God miscarry in their haste: 'I said in my haste, I am cut off, but thou heardest the voice of my supplication' (Psalm 31:22); 'I said in my haste, All men are liars' (Psalm 116:11); even Samuel and all the prophets who had assured him of the kingdom. It will come in the best time when it cometh in God's time, neither too soon nor too late; it will come sooner than your enemies would have it, sooner than second causes seem to promise, sooner than you deserve, soon enough to discover the glory of God to you: 'I waited patiently for the LORD, and he inclined unto me, and heard my cry' (Psalm 40:1). God will not fail a waiting soul; his delay is no denial, nor a sign of want of love to you:

'Jesus loved Lazarus' (John 11:5); and yet, 'When he had heard that he was sick, he abode two days still in the same place where he was' (verse 6). It may come sooner than you expect: 'When I said, My foot slippeth, thy mercy, O LORD, held me up' (Psalm 94:18). David was apt to think all was gone, help would never come more to him, and in that season God delivered him.

(3) *Obedience*: the Son of God submitted to the Holy Spirit while the impure spirit tempted him. If you would look for a ceasing of the conflict, do as he did, carry it humbly, fruitfully, faithfully to God.

(i) A humble carriage [behaviour and attitude] will become you under your conflicts: 'Humble yourselves therefore under the mighty hand of God, that he may exalt you in due time' (1 Peter 5:6). The stubbornness of the child maketh his correction double to what it otherwise would be. The more submissive you are, the more the cross hath its effect; whether you will or no, you must passively submit to God.

(ii) Carry it fruitfully [Be made the more fruitful], otherwise you obstruct the kindness of the Lord. He proveth us, that we may be fruitful: 'Every branch in me that beareth not fruit he taketh away; and every branch that beareth fruit he purgeth it, that it may bring forth more fruit' (John 15:2). The rod hath done its work when it maketh us more holy; then the comfortable days come: 'Now no chastening for the present seemeth to be joyous, but grievous; nevertheless afterward it yieldeth the peaceable fruit of righteousness unto them which are exercised thereby' (Hebrews 12:11). Righteousness brings peace along with it, inward and outward. This maketh amends for the trouble. Then God beginneth to take it off [remove the rod of correction].

(iii) Carry it faithfully [be obedient] to God, still opposing sin and Satan; for the more you give way to Satan, the more you are troubled with him, and your misery is increased, not lessened. But if you repel his temptations, he is discouraged: 'Neither give place to the devil' (Ephesians 4:27). The devil watcheth for a door to enter and take possession of your hearts, that he may exercise his former tyranny. If he gaineth any ground, he makes fearful havoc in the soul, and weakeneth not only our comfort but our grace. Therefore imitate Christ's resolution and resistance here. But this will deserve a point by itself. Therefore:

Doctrine 2. When the devil is thoroughly and resolutely resisted, he departeth.

As here, when the adversary was put to the foil [defeated], he went his way. Therefore this is often pressed upon us in scripture: 'Resist the devil, and he will flee from you' (James 4:7). If you resist his suggestions to malice, envy, and strife, he is discouraged; so 1 Peter 5:9: 'Whom resist, stedfast in the faith.' We must not fly [flee away] nor yield to him in the least, but stoutly and peremptorily resist him in all his temptations. If you stand your ground, Satan falleth. In this spiritual conflict Satan hath only weapons offensive, cunning wiles and fiery darts, none defensive; a believer hath weapons both offensive and defensive, sword and shield, etc; therefore our safety lieth in resisting.

About which is to be considered: (1) What kind of resistance this must be; (2) Arguments to persuade and enforce it; (3) What graces enable us in this resistance.

Sermon 7

1. *For the kind of resistance*
(1) It must not be faint and cold. Some kind of resistance may be made by general and common graces; the light of nature will rise up in defiance of many sins, especially at first, before men have sinned away natural light; or else the resistance at least is in some cold way. But it must be earnest and vehement, as against the enemy of God and our souls. Paul's resistance in his conflicts was with serious dislikes and deep groans: 'The good that I would I do not, but the evil which I would not, that I do' (Romans 7:9); and verse 24: 'Oh wretched man that I am! who shall deliver me from the body of this death?'

In apparent cases a detestation and vehement indignation is enough: 'Get thee behind me, Satan!'; in other cases there need strong arguments and considerations, that the temptation may not stick when the tempter is gone, as the smutch [smudge] remaineth of a candle stuck against a stone wall. When Eve speaketh faintly and coldly, the devil reneweth the assault with the more violence: 'Ye shall not eat of it, neither shall ye touch it, lest ye die' (Genesis 3:3). As to the restraint, she speaketh warmly, and with some impatience of resentment, 'not eat' 'nor touch'; in the commination [threatening] too coldly, 'lest ye die', when God had said, 'ye shall *surely* die'.

A faint denial is a kind of grant; therefore slight Satan's assaults with indignation. Though the dog barketh the traveller passeth on. Satan cannot endure contempt. At other times argue for God stoutly; thy soul and eternal concernments are in danger. No worldly concernment [consideration] ought to go so near to us as that which concerneth our eternal good and the salvation of our souls. What would the devil have from thee but thy soul, and its precious enjoyments, peace of conscience, hope of everlasting life? What doth he bid? Only worldly vanities. As the merchant putteth up [puts away] his wares [merchandise] with indignation when the chapman [pedlar] biddeth an unworthy price.

(2) It must be a thorough resistance of all sin, 'take the little foxes', dash 'Babylon's brats against the stones'. Lesser sticks set the great ones on fire. The devil cannot hope to prevail for great things presently. At first it is, 'Hath God said?' and then, 'Ye shall not surely die.' The approaches of Satan to the soul are gradual; he asketh a little, it is no great matter. Consider the evil of a temptation is better *kept* out than gotten out. Many think to stop after they have yielded a little; but when the stone at the top of a hill begins to roll downward, it is hard to stay it, and you cannot say how far you shall go. 'I'll yield but once,' saith a deceived heart; 'I'll yield but a little, and never yield again.' The devil will carry thee further and further, till he hath not left any tenderness in thy conscience. Some that thought to venture but a shilling [a small sum of money], by the witchery [addiction] of gaming [betting] have played away all [their money]. Some have sinned away all principles of conscience.

(3) It must not be for a while, but continued; not only to stand out against the first assault, but a long siege. What Satan cannot gain by argument he seeketh to gain by importunity; but 'resist him, stedfast in the faith', as his instruments spake to Joseph, 'day by day' (Genesis 39:10). Our thoughts by time are more reconciled to evil. Now we must keep up our zeal to the last. To yield at last is to lose the glory of the conflict. Therefore rate away the importunate suitor, as Christ doth.

2. *Arguments to persuade it*

(1) Because he cannot overcome you without your own consent. The wicked are 'taken captive by him at his will and pleasure' (2 Timothy 2:26), because they yield themselves to his temptations; like the young man in Proverbs 7:22: 'He goeth after her straightway, as an ox goeth to the slaughter, and as a fool to the correction of the stocks.' There is a consent, or, at least, there is not a powerful dissent. Satan's power lieth not in a constraining efficacy [sheer force], but persuasive allurement [seduction].

(2) The sweetness of victory will recompense the trouble of resistance. It is much more pleasing to deny a temptation than to yield to it; the pleasure of sin is short-lived, but the pleasure of self-denial is eternal.

(3) Grace, the more it is tried and exercised, the more it is evidenced to be right and sincere: 'Knowing that tribulation worketh patience, and patience experience, and experience hope, and hope maketh not ashamed, because the love of God is shed abroad in our hearts, by the Holy Ghost, which is given to us' (Romans 5:3-5). It is a comfortable thing to know that we are of the truth, and to be able to assure our hearts before God.

(4) Grace is strengthened when it hath stood out against a trial; as a tree shaken with fierce winds is more fruitful, its roots being loosened. Satan is a loser and you a gainer by temptations wherein you have approved your fidelity to God; as a man holdeth a stick the faster [firmer] when another seeketh to wrest [wrench] it out of his hands.

(5) The more we resist Satan, the greater will our reward be: 'I have fought a good fight, I have finished my course, I have kept the faith; henceforth there is laid up for me a crown of righteousness' (2 Timothy 4:7, 8). The danger of the battle will increase the joy of the victory, as the dangers of the way make home the sweeter. There will a time come when he that is now a soldier will be a conqueror: 'The God of peace shall bruise Satan under your feet shortly' (Romans 16:20).

(6) Where Satan gets possession, after he seemeth to be cast out, he returneth with the more violence, and tyranniseth the more: 'Then goeth he and taketh with himself seven other spirits more wicked than himself, and they enter in, and dwell there; and the last state of that man is worse than the first' (Matthew 12:45).

(7) The Lord's grace is promised to him that resisteth. God keepeth us from the evil one, but it is by our watchfulness and resistance; his power maketh it effectual. We are to strive against sin and keep ourselves, and God keepeth us by making our keeping effectual.

3. *What are the graces that enable us in this resistance?*
I answer, the three fundamental graces, faith, hope and love, so the spiritual armour is represented: 'But let us, who are of the day, be sober, putting on the breastplate of faith and love, and for an helmet the hope of salvation' (1 Thessalonians 5:8).

(1) A strong faith: 'Whom resist, stedfast in the faith' (1 Peter 5:9). This is, in the general, a sound belief of eternity, or a deep sense of the world to come: when we believe the

gospel with an assent so strong as constantly to adhere to the duties prescribed, and to venture all upon the hopes offered therein.

(2) A fervent love, arising out of the sense of our obligations to God, that we do with all readiness of mind set ourselves to do his will, levelling and directing our actions to his glory. 'Love is strong as death, and many waters cannot quench love, neither can the floods drown it' (Canticles 8:6, 7). This love will neither be bribed nor frightened from Christ.

(3) A lively hope, that doth so long and wait for glory to come, that present things do not greatly move us, either delights: 'Whom having not seen ye love, in whom, though now ye see him not, yet believing, ye rejoice with joy unspeakable and full of glory' (1 Peter 1:8); or the terrors of sense: 'For I reckon that the sufferings of this life are not worthy to be compared with the glory that shall be revealed in us' (Romans 8:18).

Doctrine 3. That those that come out of eminent conflicts are usually delivered by God in a glorious manner.

Christ was a pattern of this: 'The devil leaveth him, and behold angels came and ministered unto him'. When God delivered his people, after a long captivity, he delivered them with glory, and some kind of triumph, when he turned the Egyptian captivity: 'They borrowed of the Egyptians jewels of silver and jewels of gold and raiment. And the LORD gave the people favour in the sight of the Egyptians, so that they lent unto them such things as they required; and they spoiled the Egyptians' (Exodus 12:35, 36).

So, in the Babylonian captivity, Cyrus chargeth his

subjects, in the place where the Jews remain, to furnish them with all things necessary for their journey: 'And whosoever remaineth in any place, where he sojourneth, let the men of his place help him with silver, and with gold, and with goods, and with beasts, besides the freewill-offering for the house of God, that is in Jerusalem' (Ezra 1:4). So, in a private instance: 'And the LORD turned the captivity of Job, when he prayed for his friends; also the LORD gave Job twice as much as he had before. Then came there unto him all his brethren, and all his sisters, and all they that had been of his acquaintance before, and did eat bread with him in his house, and they bemoaned him, and comforted him over all the evil that the LORD had brought upon him; every man also gave him a piece of money, and every one an earring of gold' (Job 42:10, 11). It is said, 'The LORD turned the captivity of Job', because he had been delivered to Satan's power till the Lord set him at liberty again, and then all his friends had compassion on him, even those that had despised him before relieved him.

So Isaiah 61:7: 'For your shame you shall have double, and for confusion they shall rejoice in their portion; therefore in their land they shall possess the double, everlasting joy shall be unto them.' They should have large and eminent honour, double honour for their shame, such a reparation [recompense] would God make them for all the troubles and damages they had sustained. So, in an ordinary providence, God raiseth up comforters to his servants after all the injuries done them by Satan's instruments. And so also in spirituals; the grief and trouble that cometh by temptation is recompensed with more abundant consolation after the conquest and victory; and God delighteth to put special marks of favour upon his people that have been faithful in an hour of trial. Now God doth this for these reasons:

(1) To show the world the advantage of godliness, and close adhering to him in an hour of temptation: 'This I had, because I kept thy precepts' (Psalm 119:56). And Psalm 58:11: 'So that a man shall say, Verily there is a reward for the righteous, verily he is a God that judgeth in the earth.'

(2) To check [restrain] our diffidence [unbelief] and murmurings under trouble. Within a while and God's children will see they have no cause to quarrel with God, or repent [regret] that they were in trouble. For sometimes God giveth not only a comfortable but a glorious issue. There is nothing lost by waiting on providence; though we abide the blows of Satan for a while, yet abide them; God is, it may be, preparing the greater mercy for you: 'And it shall be said in that day, Lo, this is our God; we have waited for him, and he will save us: this is the LORD; we have waited for him, we will be glad and rejoice in his salvation' (Isaiah 25:9). Afflictions are sharp in their season, but the end is glorious.

Use

Do not always reckon upon temporal felicity [happiness]; refer that to God, but do as Jesus, who, in his sharp trials: 'For the joy that was set before him, endured the cross, despising the shame, and is set down at the right hand of the throne of God' (Hebrews 12:2, 3). There is a sure crown of life: 'Blessed is the man that endureth temptation, for when he is tried, he shall receive the crown of life, which the Lord hath promised to them that love him' (James 1:12). That is enough to content a Christian, the eternal reward is sure. In this world he shall receive with persecution an hundredfold, but in the world to come eternal life: 'There is no man that hath left house, or brethren, or sisters, or father, or mother, or wife, or children, or lands, for my sake and the gospel's, but he shall receive an hundred-fold now in this time, houses, and brethren, and sisters, and mothers, and children, and lands, with persecutions, and in the world to come eternal life' (Mark 10:29, 30).

Doctrine 4. That God maketh use of the ministry of angels in supporting and comforting his afflicted servants.

He did so to Christ, he doth so to the people of Christ. Partly for the defence and comfort of the godly: 'The angel of the LORD encampeth round about them that fear him, and delivereth them' (Psalm 34:7); 'Are they not all ministering spirits, sent forth to minister to them who shall be the heirs of salvation?' (Hebrews 1:14). Their ministry is now invisible, but yet certain. And partly also for the terror of their enemies. When David had said, 'The LORD hath chosen the hill of Sion to dwell in' (Psalm 68:16), he adds in verse 17: 'The chariots of God are twenty thousand, even thousands of angels'; implying that no kingdom in the world hath such defence, and such potent and numerous armies as the church hath, and the kingdom of Christ. God hath fixed his residence there, and the angels serve him, and attend upon him; and he will be no less terrible to his foes in Sion, that oppose the gospel, than he showed himself in Sinai, when he gave the law. Where the king is there his attendants are; so where Christ is the courtiers of heaven take up their station. Now Christ is with his church to the end of the world, therefore these thousands of angels are there, ready to be employed by him. Now we may be sure of this ministry.

(1) They delight in the preaching of the gospel, and the explication [explanation] of the mysteries of godliness:

'Which things the angels desire to look into' (1 Peter 1:12); 'To the end that now, unto the principalities and powers in heavenly places, might be known by the church the manifold wisdom of God' (Ephesians 3:10).

(2) They delight in the holy conversation of the godly, as they are offended with all impurity, filthiness and ungodliness. If good men be offended at the sins of the wicked, as 'Lot's righteous soul was vexed from day to day with their ungodly deeds' (2 Peter 2:8), much more are these holy spirits, especially when all things are irregularly carried [done unscripturally] in the worship of God: 'For this cause ought the woman to have power on her head, because of the angels' (1 Corinthians 11:10); 'I charge thee before God, and the Lord Jesus Christ, and the elect angels, that thou observe these things, without preferring one before another, doing nothing by partiality' (1 Timothy 5:21).

(3) They fight against the devil, and defend the godly in their extreme dangers. When the devil cometh into the church of God, like a wolf into the flock, they oppose and resist him. Therefore there is said to be war in heaven, that is, in the church, between Michael and his angels, and the devil and his angels: 'And there was war in heaven, Michael and his angels fought against the dragon, and the dragon fought and his angels' (Revelation 12:7). In the highest heaven there is no war. In short, the angels and believers make one church, under one head, Christ; and at length shall both live together in the same place.

Why doth God make use of the ministry of angels? And how far?

(1) To manifest unto them the greatness and glory of his work in the recovering mankind, that their delight [the angels'] in the love and wisdom of God may be increased. All holy creatures delight in any manifestation of God, the angels more especially: 'Which things the angels desire to look into' (1 Peter 1:12); 'To the intent that now, unto the principalities and powers in heavenly places, may be known by the church the manifold wisdom of God' (Ephesians 3:10). Though they themselves be not parties interested, the spectators, not the guests; yet they are delighted in the glory of God, and are kindly affectionated to the salvation of lost men; and that they may have a nearer view of this mystery, God gratifieth them by sending them often to attend upon the dispensation of the gospel, and to assist in it so far as is meet for creatures.

They [angels] are present in our assemblies: see 1 Corinthians 11:10, 1 Timothy 5:21. They see who is negligent in his office, who hindereth the preaching of the gospel; they observe what is the success of it, and when it obtaineth its effect: 'There shall be joy in heaven over one sinner that repenteth' (Luke 15:7). They are hereby more excited to praise and glorify God, and are careful to vouchsafe their attendance about the meanest that believe in him: 'He shall give his angels charge over thee, to keep thee in all thy ways. They shall bear thee up in their hands, lest thou dash thy foot against a stone' (Psalm 91:11, 12).

(2) To maintain a society and communion between all the parts of the family of God. When God gathered together the things in heaven and in earth, he brought all into subjection

and dependence upon one common head, Jesus Christ: 'That in the dispensation of the fulness of times, he might gather together in one all things in Christ, both which are in heaven, and which are on earth, even in him' (Ephesians 1:10). Men by adoption, angels by transition, are taken into the family of Christ. Now there is some intercourse [exchange of fellowship] between the several parts thereof. Our goodness extendeth not to them, but is confined to the saints on earth, in whom should be our delight; yet their help may be useful to us, they being such excellent and glorious creatures; but we are forbidden to invoke them or trust in them. God doth employ them in the affairs of his people. Their help is not the fruit of our trust in them, but their obedience to God; and it is seen in frustrating the endeavours of Satan and his instruments, and other services wherein Christ employeth them. God showed this to Jacob in the vision of the ladder, which stood upon earth, and the top reached to heaven – a figure of the providence of God, especially in and about the gospel: 'Hereafter you shall see the heaven open, and the angels of God ascending and descending upon the Son of man' (John 1:51); to carry on the work of the gospel, and to promote the glory and interest of Christ's kingdom in the world. Thus far in the general we may be confident of.

(3) To preserve his people from many dangers and casualties, which fall not within the foresight of man, God employeth 'the watchers', as they are called in Daniel 4:13 and 17, for he is tender of [concerned for] his people, and doth all things by proper means. Now the angels having a larger foresight than we, they are appointed to be guardians. This they do according to God's pleasure, preventing many

dangers, which we could by no means foresee. They observe the devil in all his walks [travels], and God useth them to prevent his sudden surprisals of his [God's] people, as [of which] instances are many.

(4) Because they are witnesses of the obedience and fidelity of Christ's disciples, and, so far as God permitteth, they cannot but assist them in their conflicts. Thus Paul in 1 Corinthians 4:9: 'We are made a spectacle unto the world, and to angels and to men'. Now the angels, that are witnesses to their combats and sufferings, cannot but make report to God: 'Take heed that ye despise not one of these little ones, for I say unto you, that in heaven their angels do always behold the face of my Father which is in heaven' (Matthew 18:10). The angels which are appointed by God to be their guardians have their continual recourses, and returns to God's glorious presence. Now, being so high in God's favour, and having continual access to make their requests and complaints known to him, they will not be silent in [on] the behalf of their fellow-servants, that either the trial may be lessened, or grace sufficient may be given to them.

(5) They do not only keep off hurt, but there are many blessings and benefits that we are partakers of by their ministry. As the angel of the Lord delivered Peter out of prison: 'And behold the angel of the Lord came upon him, and a light shined in the prison; and he smote Peter on the side, and raised him up, saying, Arise up quickly; and his chains fell off from his hands ...' (Acts 12:7). But he doth not give thanks to the angel, but to God: 'Now I know of a surety that the Lord hath sent his angel, and hath delivered me

...'(verse 11). He directeth it to God, not to the creature. The angels do us many favours; all the thanks we do them is that we do not offend them by our sins against God; other gratitude they expect not.

(6) Their last office is at death and judgment. In death, to convey our souls to Christ: 'And it came to pass that the beggar died, and was carried by the angels into Abraham's bosom' (Luke 16:22); that so we may enjoy our rest in heaven. In the last day they will gather the bodies of Christ's redeemed ones from all parts of the world, after they have been resolved into dust, and mingled with the dust of other men, that every saint may have his own body again, wherein he hath obeyed and glorified God: 'And he shall send his angels with a great sound of a trumpet, and they shall gather together his elect from the four winds, from one end of heaven to the other' (Matthew 24:31). That is, from all parts and quarters of the world, that their souls may return to their old beloved habitations, and then both in body and in soul they may be for ever with the Lord.

Use

Now this is a great comfort to the church and people of God, when the powers and principalities on earth are employed against them, to consider what powers and principalities attend upon Christ. We serve such a master as hath authority over the holy angels, to employ them at his pleasure; and in their darkest condition his people feel the benefit of it. As the angel of the Lord appeared to Paul in a dreadful storm: 'There stood by me this night the angel of the Lord, whose I am, and whom I serve, saying, Fear not, Paul ...' (Acts 27:23, 24). So to Christ in his agonies: 'There appeared an angel to him from heaven strengthening him' (Luke 22:43). So against Satan, the good angels are ready to comfort us, as the evil angels are ready to trouble and tempt us. Let us then look to God, at whose direction they are sent to help and comfort us.

Doctrine 5. If God taketh away ordinary helps from us, he can supply us by means extraordinary, as he did Christ's hunger by the ministry of angels. Therefore till God's power be wasted there is no room for despair. We must not limit the Holy One of Israel to our ways and means, as they did: 'They turned back, and tempted God, and limited the Holy One of Israel' (Psalm 78:41).